T0171420

Ancient Secrets of the Goddesses

Velva Dawn Silver-Hughes

BALBOA.
PRESS
A DIVISION OF HAY HOUSE

Balboa Press books may be ordered through booksellers or by contacting:

Balboa Press
A Division of Hay House
1663 Liberty Drive
Bloomington, IN 47403
www.balboapress.com
1-(877) 407-4847

ISBN: 978-1-4525-3858-7 (sc)
ISBN: 978-1-4525-3859-4 (hc)
ISBN: 978-1-4525-3857-0 (e)

Library of Congress Control Number: 2011915023

Cover Art by J. Steven High www.bigharts1.com

Back Cover Author Photo by Visual Hues Photography Inc.
www.visualhues.com

Print information available on the last page.

Balboa Press rev. date: 2/23/2015

Contents

To my mom, Velva Kay Frances Silver, thank you for being one of my greatest teachers. Thank you for your unconditional love, wisdom, and teachings, and for choosing me.

To each of the goddesses for sharing their ancient wisdom enabling us to truly embrace the divine feminine.

Introduction

Messages from the Goddesses

The Goddessses have been waiting many years for these words of wisdom to be collected in this magical book. This book contains the energy of thirty-three goddesses combined with the life experiences and healings from our sister goddess Velva Dawn. One of Velva Dawn's life purposes is to help awaken the ancient wisdom and energy of the divine feminine to balance the universal energies of the masculine and feminine. You may already be feeling the awakening of the female divine presence within your soul. This book is a combination of healing stories shared from Velva Dawn's heart from her wisdom of this life and the many years of past life experiences that she has had.

We want this book to ignite the goddess flame within each of you, heal wounds from this lifetime and past lifetimes, nurture your soul, give you the tools to use in your life to move forward on your true life path and to follow and know the true essence of your soul. Each goddess has many qualities that when revealed in this book will bring magical healings to ones soul, awakening the feminine magic that has been lying dormant for years!

We are very honored that this knowledge is coming forth now in perfect divine time. Before you start to read this book, sit down quietly for a moment and write down some goals that you wish to achieve or wounds that you may want to heal, whatever it is that you want to manifest out of light and love. Put those intentions on a piece of paper, fold this paper, and put it in the back pages of this book. Please be sure to write a date on your sheet of paper and then sit back and enjoy the process of allowing your imagination to flow with the energy of the book.

You will find yourself healing along with Velva Dawn's stories and the nurturing of the goddesses within each chapter of this book.

Each person who reads this book has been divinely guided to do so and will heal all that he or she wish upon this magical journey.

This book is multidimensional and will heal you on many different levels. The words have been vibrationally toned to shift blocks in your chakras, and you may strongly feel each goddess as you shift your way through the book. You may even see the colors of the goddesses as you get to know them and can amplify your manifestations and healing using the crystals that are associated with each goddess. To get the maximum healing, you may wish to take your time while reading this book. Read a chapter, and then take a few days to connect with each goddess. Practice using her words of wisdom in your daily life, really try to absorb all of her energies into your chakras and trust in the process of the divine feminine. This book was written at the vibration of love and light amplified for healing, joy, wisdom, and nurturing that each soul agrees to with this book.

You may see the book magically opening up and all of the goddesses lovingly reaching out to heal you on every level, if this is what you wish for.

Chapter 1

Isis

Balance

Color: Royal Blue
Crystal: Lapis Lazuli

It all began centuries ago with a woman who called herself Isis. She was a special deity whose primary characteristic was to teach women, both younger than herself and older, how to retain and ignite their inner goddesses. She can teach you how to balance life as a goddess, a wife, a mother, and a sister, and to always remember that your inner goddess is the most important aspect of every woman's life. Isis could see that many women would give up what they wanted in life once they chose to marry the loves of their lives, and more so, to delve into motherhood and to dote on everyone's needs but theirs. Isis wishes to share her secrets of how she balanced all of these very important essences within her own life.

I was the daughter of a very powerful man in Egypt. From the time I was a little girl, I was being sculpted and guided to take on my regal role later in life. I was taught by my mother and her sisters how to ignite the inner sorceress within my soul and use it for light and love with those whom I felt guided to help. I would start each day with an intention for myself that I wished to learn more about during the day, invoking a lesson in which I needed to serve myself better. Not enough women today even know what they want in life, let alone ask for what they wish to manifest . . . why is that? I feel that we have lost the feminine energy that once served and honored all of the goddesses from ancient times. So this is the reason that I am asking Velva Dawn to speak out for me. I see an energy shift coming very soon, and I know that my lifetime lessons can help other women serve their lives' purposes with passion, commitment, joy, fulfillment, love, and harmony. It seems to me that women are either really career focused or are stay-at-home mothers, raising their children. Now I did have servants to help me with my house chores and children, but that doesn't mean that each and every one of you can't manifest divine intentions also. Wake up each morning and ask yourself, "What do I want to do today, and what can I do that will fill my inner child with joy and light?"

Do you feel you deserve to ask for what you want? Deep down inside, a lot of women don't feel worthy of asking for what they truly desire. In this chapter, we are going to ignite that sleeping inner goddess who has been lying dormant for centuries within each and every one of you! Yes, you each have an inner goddess.

Let's start by finding a quiet place where you can have some short time alone, fifteen to twenty minutes at the most for a start.

You can either lie down or sit in a cross-legged position. Place eight clear quartz crystals in a circle around you. Then please put a lapis lazuli in the center of the circle and hold an amethyst in each hand. Invoke the goddess Isis, asking her to help guide the awakening of the inner goddess celebration. Ask for your spirit guides, guardian angels, and Archangel Michael to watch over and protect your space during this time. Now close your eyes and slowly start listening to your breath, inhaling slowly and then exhaling at the same rate. Repeat this breathing technique for a count of twenty. Feel the crown of your head open up wide to the heavens, and feel the magical divine energy flowing into your crown. Send your roots from the soles of your feet, thanking Mother Earth for her gift of life. Once you feel that your roots are deeply connected and you can feel the energy tingling up your legs, focus on your solar plexus. Envision the sunshine opening up your power center and expanding this center to be bright yellow sunshine. Keep breathing as you allow these centers to fully open. Trust that all is well and that you are fully protected during this special ceremony. Then feel your heart center filling up with an emerald green light from Archangel Raphael, healing all past life issues and balancing all karmic ties for this or any past lives that need to be healed. Isis is still with you; she is asking you to keep breathing deeply. Breathe through any pain that you might have and ask her to assist in decreasing any painful breaths you might encounter.

Envision Isis holding her magic blue lapis lazuli healing wand, see her touching your solar plexus with this special tool, and feel the instant igniting of the goddess flame within your solar plexus. See this flame getting higher and brighter, shining with a vibrant yellow, orange, and red flame, burning with a purple tip on the top of the flame.

Feel your power growing and expanding. Does this trigger any memories from any past lives where you were very powerful as a higher priestess or a goddess? Look at that lifetime for a brief period. Where were you? Who were you married to? Did you have any children? What were you doing in that lifetime? If you see that you were not using your energy for love and light in that lifetime, know that in this lifetime you are here to spread love and light to the universe; it's okay to be powerful this time. Mother Earth needs your help to spread divine healing energy around the world to help with the energy shift that is coming soon. Embrace your power, feel it, and breathe it deeply into your solar plexus; feel the passion in your sacral and root chakras. During this time, think of something that you would like to accomplish in this lifetime for yourself, for your family, for the world.

Breathe in these intentions and ask Isis to help guide you and give you the strength and wisdom that you will need to follow through with your goals. She is there with you now and will remain by your side, gently giving you what you need to fulfill your life's purposes. She is there to help you if you are in a marriage that is abusive or that just isn't right for you. Lean on her and ask her for what you need at any given time. She will lend her strong, wise hands to help you through the hard times, and she will be there to celebrate the joys in your life. Once you feel that you have fully ignited the inner goddess flame and have stated your intention for love and light, slowly bring your awareness back into your body, wiggling your fingers and toes. Slowly breathing in and out, gently open your eyes. If you are feeling dizzy, be sure to put your roots down into Mother Earth again, asking for her help to ground your energy. How do you feel? Do you feel powerful and full of creative energy? Each and every time you do this meditation, you can state a different intention.

Isis has been called forth to help women in this century fulfill their wishes and create a more balanced, loving energy within the world. We need to have more of a universal feminine and masculine ebb and flow. The world has had a stronger masculine energy, and this has created many ego wars within and surrounding all. We need to send love out to each and every person living on the Earth and to all beings of love and light. We are moving into a world of transcendence. People will be communicating by using ESP and making decisions according to their intuition. We communicated in Egypt using our sacred intuition in all aspects of our lives. We focused on what needed to be done right at that moment. We used our energies to heal ourselves and to heal one another. We used the Earth, crystals, herbs, and geometric shapes and patterns to heal and facilitate all aspects of life. We used energies in ways that one thought impossible. We opened our awareness completely and trusted totally in the divine. We moved large stones to build our sacred pyramids. We lived our lives by divine guidance, following it and never questioning. We took the time daily, sometimes hourly, to center ourselves and ask our inner goddesses what would serve our highest intention for the day. We manifested our intentions for the day knowing that all other tasks would easily be completed if we followed our divine paths for the day.

Trust that the balance will flow harmoniously if you put out your true intentions of love and light first thing in the morning, taking some time to celebrate and connect with your soul. Allow your inner goddesses to dance and sing and move freely throughout the day, listening to her gentle wisdom guiding you as to what would be best for your body. She will help you with healthy eating if you ask her to. She wants your body to be full of high-energy fruits, vegetables, low-fat proteins, lots of pure water, and healing gem elixirs. She knows that your body will function at its utmost ability if you feed it with sacred foods, water, and movement. Cherish your body as your own holy temple. Ask your inner goddess what serves her best. Listen to her true divine answers every time you go to eat or drink. Ask her if this is serving your true higher self or if you are feeding your ego.

Once you start listening to this feminine voice, she will carry you with grace and dignity throughout your life. She wants you to live with integrity, wisdom, happiness, love, abundance, and total completeness within your sacred temple.

The woman that I dedicate this chapter to is Eira Germaine Silver. She was my grandmother, a woman who was a pioneer in her time. My grandma lived only a couple of hundred feet from my home when I was growing up on our family farm. I was raised on a generational mixed farm with grain and cattle. I loved to visit my grandma's house. The amazing memories I have of her are plentiful. When I was a young girl, in the summertime I always loved to help her make homemade crab apple jelly. I would go up the ladder and pick the ripe crab apples, putting them into an ice cream bucket. When we had enough apples picked, then we would go inside her house and start the process of making jelly. I loved the smell of the jelly as it was cooking! She would make homemade bread the old-fashioned way and we would put the freshly made crab apple jelly on the warm bread . . . Is your mouth watering as mine is?

My grandma loved to have a garden full of fresh vegetables and flowers! She grew many colorful sweet peas and gladiolus;

I would be the first one out in her front yard smelling the sweet peas and asking her if I could cut some and make her an arrangement. Every year I grow sweet peas and fondly think of those memories with her.

Eira also taught me how to iron my granddad's checked cloth hankies. I took so much pride in ironing those red and blue square hankies that he would use each day. He too was a very important man in my childhood and life. My granddad was from Scotland and so my grandma would make his mother's recipe for Scottish bannocks. We would all sit around and have tea and fresh bannocks.

As I grew older, my grandma would tell me stories of how her mother told her that she should have a career and her schooling completed before she got married, in case her marriage didn't work out. Then she would have a way to support herself and her children. Imagine a woman thinking that independently!

So my grandma was one of the first women to graduate from the University of Edmonton with her diploma in nursing in 1937.

My grandma was eleven years younger than my grandfather and they had met when she was just eight years old and he was seventeen years old. My grandfather knew that she was too young to marry so he had to wait until she was much older.

Once my grandmother graduated and worked for a year, she then married my granddad and quit her job as a nurse. She had four children and was a full-time homemaker, and much more!

My grandma gave me her old nursing books as I had a medical background and she thought that I would enjoy them. I treasure these books and am so grateful to have them. I remember talking with her and telling her how amazed I was that she took all of that schooling and then only used it for a year. She told me that it was more important that she was around to raise her family and that her schooling was just a back up if she needed it!

I am so grateful to have had such a wise woman living so close to me. She was full of love to give, she had the patience to teach me many crafts, and she unconditionally loved me even though I was adopted. I always felt true love from her.

I feel that it is important for a young girl to have such a balanced role model in her life, just as Isis guided many young women so long ago.

Using Shapes to Protect and Clear Yourself and Your Home

Isis used many different geometric shapes to help her throughout her life path. The pyramid shape can be used to clear any negative energy in your auric field. Envision a pyramid shape around the outside of your body and ask that any negative energy that comes into your auric field be transmuted into love and light, and then send it up through the top of the pyramid to the heavens to be recycled. You can also used this pyramid shape over your home to protect it, your vehicle, your family, pets, or whatever you wish to protect.

I have found lately that I need to use different shapes for protection, as my old ways of using colors for protection were not working as efficiently with the shifting energy fields of the present. One of the shapes that I like to use is the octahedron. I envision it around myself and that all eight sides of the crystalline structure will bounce off any negative energy that comes within or near my auric field. You may even envision a certain color of crystal to have the healing quality of that crystal in your auric field. You can also add a pyramid around the octahedron for extra protection. When you are going to public places with a lot of different energies it is best to use both methods if you feel guided to do this, and you may envision the octahedron being a hematite with a few clear quartz windows to see all. Trust your instincts on this and use whatever shape you are guided to use.

Remember that if you don't protect yourself from negative energy then you may eventually fill up your auric field with negative energy and disease can set in. You are the only one who can take care of your auric field daily. So take the time to do this for yourself. If you aren't healthy, then who will take care of you and/or your family members?

Isis is a goddess of many dimensions. She will teach you how to balance your life in all ways if you ask her. It is possible to have it all with balance and divine trust.

Isis's gift to every woman who reads this chapter is harmony fulfilled with love, power, wisdom, and abundance in her physical, spiritual, emotional, and etheric realms of life. Envision these qualities in a golden, wrapped gift from one goddess to another. When you are guided slowly, take the time to unwrap these divine tools for your daily life. Each person's gift will be unique and divinely timed. You may wish to journal your gifts from Isis and then take some time to get to know the energy of each tool and when you can use it in your daily life tasks.

Crystal Healing

You may place the lapis lazuli crystal on your third eye or above your crown chakra to stimulate a new understanding of spiritual maturity. Lapis lazuli will assist you with awakening your third eye, allowing you to harmonize your inner visions with your physical world. This crystal will also give you the gift of self-knowledge, which is one of the greatest paths we will follow while on Earth. You may also wish to amplify the healing of Isis by placing the lapis lazuli crystal in a glass pitcher of spring water overnight during a full moon. Ask Isis to bring her essence into the elixir with her magical qualities that will benefit you the most.

Affirmation

"Bless each goddess with all dimensions of infinite wisdom to enable them to create a more harmonious loving energy on Earth."

Dedication:

This chapter is dedicated to Grandma Eira Germaine Silver. Thank you for being such a strong, wise, loving, and independent woman! You have inspired many!

Eira Germaine Silver
Graduation Photo
Diploma in Nursing
University of Edmonton
1937

Chapter 2

———— ⚜ ————

Mother Mary
Self-Love

Color: Rose Pink
Crystal: Rose Quartz

I am the goddess that spreads love and teaches you how to nurture yourself.

Women need to give love to themselves so that they can be of true service to their loved ones and career choices. When we are constantly giving energy to others and we forget to fill up our own glasses, we run into trouble and start feeling bitter and resentful toward the very people whom we love the most. We need to take a little time each and every day to open our heart centers and fill ourselves up with love. We need to look into the mirror every day and say to our true inner goddess, "I love you," and we need to repeat this affirmation daily. We each have an inner child that needs to be loved and craves joy! We forget that we are human and not robots and that we need to have some positive affirmations toward ourselves and our loving self-image.

Mother Mary said that in her time women did not have the self-image issues that we have today. In ancient times, they followed their divine guidance to live their lives. They listened to their inner child and honored him or her by doing what he or she needed at the time. When one does not truly love oneself, then one can't truly love another.

Filling Up Your Cup

You may wish to begin each day by asking yourself this question: what do I love most about myself today? What can I do today that will fill my heart with joy? There is always one thing that you can find to love about yourself, and if you need help then ask your loved ones and they will surely help you out. We are too hard on ourselves and are most likely our worst critics. There are many ways that we can naturally fill up our souls and release any pain that our bodies are ready to release. Remember when you are feeling an emotion or pain that it is your body's way of telling you it is time to release these old paradigms and vibrations; the next step is being willing to ask the divine for help in letting go.

Take the time to listen to your body. Have a five—to ten-minute nap if you feel tired; the dishes will be there later to put away or wash. Get a massage if your back is aching instead of self-medicating with analgesics, and watch the sunset to help tone your sacral chakra, which will spike your creativity and passion. Go outside during a full moon and ask Sister Luna's rays to infuse your body and to clear all of your chakras and your auric field.

You can go outside and lie on the ground, inviting Mother Earth's energy into your body and feeling her pulse within your soul. You can find an inviting tree that you are guided to merge energies with and ask permission to hug that tree and to receive some healing energy from a living being. You see, we are all living creatures of this Earth and God wants us to be as one—one breath all in harmony with the universe, a total ebb and flow, inhaling divine healing and exhaling toxic energy if need be. We need to remember, as infinite beings, that we are all capable of miracles and that we can heal ourselves. We just need to slow down and listen to what our bodies are trying to tell us. What are you hearing? What is that sore shoulder trying to tell you? Listen to it . . .

Mother Mary is often said to be an extra guardian angel overseeing the raising of adopted children. I am an adopted child. I remember when I was about five or six years old my adoptive parents told me that I was a chosen daughter to them. They told me that they chose me because I was special. I am very fortunate that they used this term to tell me about being adopted, as I always felt special growing up. As I grew older, I started to understand more of the process that everyone who was involved must have had to experience emotionally. I did start to feel really sad on my birthday, wondering why my birth mother and birth father gave me up for adoption. What was the real story that took place between them?

As an adoptee, you are only given one sheet of paper that gives you the hair color, height, weight, interests, and dislikes of your biological parents. So I did not have a lot of information to gather my visual image of what my birth mother or father might look like. I did not look similar to my adopted mother or father or adopted brother. I would walk down the street always looking for someone who might look similar to me.

I was fortunate to have had such amazing adopted parents and grandparents. I grew up on a combined farm near a small hamlet in Alberta. By *combined farm* I mean that my family had cattle and we were also grain farmers. I feel very lucky to have grown up on a farm learning how to care for animals of all types, growing a garden for fruits and vegetables, mowing the lawn, camping outdoors, learning how to make crab-apple jelly from my grandma, long walks picking rocks with my granny, learning how to iron my granddad's cloth handkerchiefs, making Scottish bannocks, smelling sweet peas growing the summer, and so much more.

There were many times in my teen years that I had close calls to harming myself. I survived all of those experiences and I know it was because Mother Mary was watching over me, guiding me to the light to keep me safe, and loving me unconditionally through thick and thin.

When I was pregnant with my first daughter, I was twenty-six years old and I started to think about how difficult it must have been for my birth mother to give me up for adoption. I started to wonder what her delivery was like, if there were any familial diseases or congenital anomalies in her family. I felt that I was closer to her then than I ever had been in my life.

I searched for an adoption search agency and in Calgary found one that I felt would be reliable. I had registered with the Post

Adoption Registry with the Alberta government and had heard nothing from that search, so I decided to go ahead and sign the consent forms. I paid my registration fees for the social worker to begin the process of finding out where my life had originated.

The social worker phoned me and told me that she had received my adoption file from the government. My birth families lived in Calgary and my birth mother did not want to give me up for adoption, but when my birth grandfather found out that she was pregnant he wanted her to have an abortion and insisted that she move out of the house. So this would explain why I have always had very strong antiabortion feelings; if my birth mother had listened to her father, I would have had a different physical body and been a different person.

The social worker told me that she had to make a few phone calls to try to get a current phone number for my birth mother. She also had to get her permission before she could release her name to me. As you can imagine, I anxiously waited for her to get this information. In the meantime, I kept my adoptive parents informed of the whole birth-parent search, including all of the newly released details so that they also felt included in this process.

Then I received the phone call that I had waited for most of my adult life. The social worker gave me my birth mother's phone number and told me that she was really looking forward to hearing from me, and that she had hoped I would look for her one day and want to have a relationship with her. When I heard my birth mother's voice for the first time, it sounded very similar to my voice. It was a very emotional phone call. We agreed to meet at a specific restaurant in Calgary; she told me what she would be wearing so I would know who she was. At this point in my life, I had already given birth to my first daughter, Kayla Dawn. So my husband Stephen, Kayla and I drove into Calgary to meet my birth mother.

As soon as I walked in the door of the restaurant, I looked over and I could see this woman who looked very similar to me but was shorter and more petite. I walked over to her and our eyes met. We both knew that we had reconnected after twenty-six years. She held my face in her hands and cried, saying that she was happy I wanted to find her and that she had missed me. The social worker had really counseled me on putting up healthy boundaries when meeting my birth parents and figuring out how this new relationship might fit into my life.

At first I thought I would be satisfied in just seeing my birth parents from across the room—just to see why I looked the way I did—but after meeting her I decided that I did want a relationship with her and her family. But I was not sure how that relationship would look at that moment.

My birth mother told me that my birth father also lived in Calgary and that he wanted to meet me, if this was of interest to me. I knew that I wanted to meet him, but I needed a bit of time to process meeting her. She gave me his phone number and I tucked it away for a few weeks and then I decided to give him a phone call. I found out during this whole process that my birth grandfather was the chief executive officer of the hospital where I was born and that he had helped to arrange my government adoption.

My birth father also wanted to meet me so that we could see each other. We met at a restaurant and sat and talked for a few hours about what his life was like when I was born. I was very loved by everyone, but the best choice for everyone involved was for me to be given up for adoption.

My birth mom was seventeen years old when I was born and my birth dad was twenty-one years old. My birth mom told me that she never ever got over the fact that she gave me up for adoption and that she wanted to go back to the hospital and take me back but her sisters helped her get through those rough, emotional postpartum blues. I could not even imagine the emotions that she must have gone through, knowing that she may never see me again and trusting that I would go to a loving home.

Both my birth mother and birth father had other children and I have relationships with most of them. I have put up boundaries around important holidays. These occasions are spent with my adoptive parents because they are my parents.

I was guided by Mother Mary to channel a guided meditation using crystals programmed by her to help heal the hearts of adopted children and birth parents.

I thought I had healed the wounds of being adopted and the feelings of abandonment until I started to channel the meditation from Mother Mary. I was overlooking the ocean from my hotel room on the Kohala Coast in Hawaii. The tears were streaming down my face, dripping on my laptop keyboard. I could feel my heart chakra aching and releasing the deep emotional wounds of the adoption process.

Mother Mary told me that I had been adopted in many lifetimes and that my birth mother agreed to carry me in her womb and to give me up for adoption so I could be with my adoptive parents who would raise me to learn the lessons that I agreed to learn in this lifetime. When I understood that my birth mother and I had this sacred contract, I felt as though I had healed my soul on many levels. I am truly grateful to my birth mother and birth father for creating my life, and to my adoptive parents for choosing me to be their daughter. I feel very blessed to have these four souls in my life. I am also very grateful to Mother Mary for watching over me, keeping me safe, and for healing my soul!

Mother Mary is the goddess who will help you heal the deep wounds in your soul no matter how big or small they are. She is there for you. She loves you unconditionally and is wanting you to love yourself as she loves you. When you are feeling sad or lonely, ask her to wrap her loving arms around you and you will feel her warm embrace filling up your heart.

I have also asked Mother Mary to help me with my healing sessions with clients, and I quite often will feel drops of water on my feet or hands. This is her giving me affirmation that she is assisting with the healing session.

Crystal Healing

You may wish to place the pink rose quartz crystal upon your heart chakra during meditation or while sleeping. The rose quartz crystal represents the heart of Mother Earth, the very core of her soul. Rose quartz offers the vibration of love, with its water element able to calm and cool any fire energy that may be present in your heart chakra.

It will assist you in letting go of old anger and fear by healing any emotional wounds in your heart from this lifetime or past lifetimes. This stone allows us to connect to the divine while being in our physical bodies. This crystal will also help reveal any areas of love that you are unconsciously blocking.

Affirmation

"Are you in the obligation vibration? Remember it is very important to love yourself first and fill up your own cup and then you can spread the vibration of universal love."

Dedication

This chapter is dedicated to my friend Sherry Martini . . . love

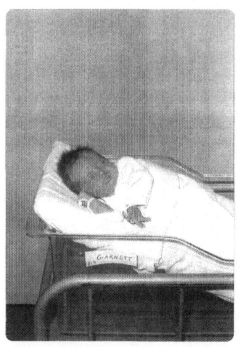

This is a photo of me a few days after I was born.
My birth mother gave this to me when I met
her . . . precious.

Chapter 3

Dana

Ancient Wisdom

Color: Pale Blue
Crystal: Avalon Blue Andara

It is time for the world to wake up and feel the knowing that each person has inside of them. The time is now to speak truths and allow them to freely flow through your body and mind. Feel your divine magic come through your soul connection pulsing through your energy body and speaking your wisdom through teachings in all aspects of your life. Communicate with the birds and animals to make this world a better place for all beings of love and light.

At the time of Avalon, we were all higher priestesses of deep knowing and we used that for our highest good. The darkness was coming and we were trying to keep this from happening for years and years, but the magic was not being used for light and love. The darkness was coming so we chose. It was time for the sisters to go beneath the waters and the time to rise is now; the time is now sisters.

Many of us had past lives in Avalon and we need to use our ancient innate wisdom in this lifetime and lifetimes to come. Communicating with animals was a natural way of life for us. When we were out in nature, the birds would follow us and give us messages about the weather, the future comings, and solutions to problems that we had. Yes, it looked like Cinderella—working goddesses surrounded by birds, deer, rabbits, foxes, dogs, and many more animals gently guiding us if we asked them for help with our life's problems or solutions for ailments.

How this communication would work was that the birds, for example, would tap an object with their beak or their feet and we could feel the vibration in our souls and we could then interpret the words. The communication wasn't in English as we speak to each other today: it wasn't even ESP. It was on a vibrational level to the soul, a true soul to soul connection.

Dana's message to all of us is this: "We need to spend more time outdoors in the natural elements to clear our auric fields and heal our physical bodies. We need to connect with Mother Earth and allow her to recycle our negative and lower vibrations of guilt, fear, jealously, rage, etc. We spend too much time indoors under artificial lighting and energy; we need to live where we really want to, so that we will love to be outdoors. Our energy body craves to be in nature. We need to honor this feeling and we will be universally more harmonious. The world will be changing as we know it. It will become more tropical and warmer with lots of trees with fruits growing on them. This will be changing starting in the year 2015. The world as we know it will change.

We can ask Mother Earth to aid us in all of our issues and queries. If you feel an ache somewhere, find a quiet, peaceful spot outside, if possible, to lie down on the grass under a tree. Ask Mother Earth to recycle your pain.

We need to ask for help more and let our ego diminish its power over our thoughts. In our past lives in Avalon, we used nature to nurture our souls. Mother Earth supplied our food sources naturally with no preservatives or artificial ingredients. We also grew plentiful gardens of herbs, flowers, fruits, and vegetables. We caught our fresh fish from the water for our protein source. Our world is so different now, you think, but it is your mission now to help Mother Earth and Mawu (Earth goddess) to assist with the change in the vibration of the Earth, which will, in effect, make this world a better place for us all to live. Positive thinking is the first step. Taking care of the Earth, recycling, growing gardens, walking, or biking to work, meditating—all of these ideas will make a huge impact on the Earth. So let's start now."

Now that you have ignited your goddess flame from the previous chapter, you can ask Dana to help you in your daily life by giving you the gifts of wisdom. Ask Dana to help you with your career, your children, your love life, and/or your finances. Ask her anything, and she will help you access the innate wisdom within.

Meditation from Dana

Discovering Your Inner Knowledge, Your Own Infinite Library

To begin, please find a comfortable spot to sit down or lie down if possible. If you can find a spot outside in nature where you can be upon an area of green grass or the sand as that would be the optimum conditions for this meditation. Once upon your area, please remember to first ask Mother Earth for permission to receive healing from her, and to thank her for life and healing. You could also find a quiet secluded place near a river or stream to do this session. Just find an area in nature where you can be alone for a minimum of thirty minutes.

Also for this healing, if you can get a dozen yellow roses that are fresh and are from a store that has amazing energy, they will amplify the healing of this meditation. Yellow is the color of power and will restore the divine wisdom within your solar plexus.

Place nine of the yellow roses in a circle where you will either sit or lie down in the center. Start at the top of the circle, at twelve o'clock, with the first flower or top of the rose facing inward so that the stem will be the perimeter of your circle.

Continue clockwise to lay the roses in a circle, with nine of the heads of the roses facing the same direction.

Then please place the flower side of the first three roses that you have left upon your chest toward your head so you can smell the beautiful rose scent while you are doing this healing. The rose will be lying vertically on your chest.

Then hold one yellow rose in each hand, as you would naturally hold a rose, and begin by asking your guardian angels, Archangel Michael, the goddess Artemis and all divine beings of love and light to protect you while doing this healing session.

Close your eyes and start to notice your breath. Take a very deep inhalation and hold it for five seconds, and then exhale deeply with a sigh to release any tension or fear that you might have. Repeat this again: inhale slowly and then exhale.

Now I want you to see yourself in a land full of green meadows and yellow butterflies flying all around. Invite Dana to help with this healing session and any other beings of love and light that you feel guided to call upon during this time. Feel your heart gently beating and share your love with Mother Earth. Send your infinite love to nature and feel her send it back to you. Then please see your infinite love connecting to the heavens and Father Sky, feeling him connecting to you.

Now you are connected to the Divine Father and Mother Earth, and you are protected in a pyramid of love.

Ask Dana and her higher priestesses to encircle you with their love and feel them gently caressing your aura and energy bodies to heal any karma from past lives. They will check your goddess flame to make sure that it is burning brightly within your solar plexus. Dana will go into your past life, when you were a powerful goddess, and will retrieve that ancient wisdom to reconnect it to your soul and to clear any fears that you might have about the having power.

She reminds you that you are powerful and that you have a library of all knowing wisdom deep within your soul.

When you have a question, all you need to do is center yourself and ask what it is that you need to know, and then sit and patiently hear the answer. It will always be there. Just listen for it.

Dana works gently on your solar plexus with the higher priestesses allowing you to feel your wisdom and power in a loving and gentle way. She pulls away any cords or intertwined webs of lower energy that may still be present.

She will gently give you any messages that you are asked to share with others or just for yourself.

She will then place a pewter-colored crown that has Celtic encryption. It means, "You are a wise goddess full of light. Please use your wisdom for love my sister."

The crown has a large oval-shaped, yellow citrine stone on the front center, embellished with two diamond-shaped lapis lazuli on either side. All of the stones are encompassed with several clear quartz crystals to amplify your wisdom and to access higher dimensions of energy.

You may then hear Dana whisper these words as this crown is placed upon your head: "You are a goddess. Use your wisdom for the light and don't be afraid of your power."

You now have this crown of energy on your head always, or you may take it off and store it in a sacred place and use it when you need it. Please know that you are wise, loving, and powerful. You are a sister to Dana and to all sisters of the world.

Now please slowly take some deep breaths to connect your roots into Mother Earth again, and you may wish to thank Dana and her higher priestesses for their healing session with you.

When I first started to bring forth and awaken my higher priestess knowledge, I wasn't fully confident in my work. This will be a work in progress where you will receive ideas to make new healing methods or teachings that others haven't written about yet. You will receive this information and then you may doubt yourself when your lower self kicks in. When I was guided to make my first healing meditation CD and started getting the words from the goddesses, I was very unsure of myself. The goddesses have been very persistent with me, pushing me to keep writing down this information and then sharing it when I am guided to do so. The biggest lesson for me from Dana is to *trust* when one is being guided by the light and one's intention is to heal others with a loving vibration that is the vibration of information that one will receive. When I was guided to program crystal kits to accompany the goddess meditations, I was so excited to do this as I have a passion for working with crystals. Combining this with the channeling of the wisdom to the vibration of Mark Watson's Angel Earth Music was a great healing tool. Mark has channeled the music for each goddess in my meditations, which amplifies the vibration of the CD.

As I move forth on my path, I can see how all of the tools and information that I am bringing forward work in combination with each other. It has taken a lot of trust on my part to follow through with these intuitive ideas. I am so glad that I stepped through my fear to bring forth this ancient wisdom because the healings that I hear about are resulting from people who are doing my work. That is all the reward I need to keep moving through any obstacles or fear that might show up along my path. Trust in yourself; you are capable of miracles.

Crystal Healing

You may wish to place the Avalon blue andara crystal on your third-eye chakra or crown chakra as this crystal will awaken the higher priestess energy from your past lives. Ask that only the knowledge of love and light containing a high vibration be brought forth. Ask Dana to help with this process. You will receive as much as you are ready to receive for each meditation session with this crystal. This crystal holds the mother energy taking you back in time when your royal blood lines began. Please give thanks to Dana and the crystal for these healing sessions.

Affirmation

"You are capable of bringing forth ancient wisdom to help with your planetary sacred contract in this lifetime."

Dedication

This chapter is dedicated to my lifetime friend, Leah Carter.

Chapter 4

~~~◦◦◦⟡◦◦◦~~~

Pele
Passion

Color: Red
Crystal: Cuprite or Divine Fire Andara

*Every woman has a divine passion in every lifetime
and it is important to find and feel that energy to fulfill
your physical and spiritual body completely.*

*I am known as the goddess of the volcanoes in Hawaii.
I have a fiery spirit creating and stirring passionate
energy within your soul."*

*In this book I want to give women the tools to find that
fiery yet peaceful energy and allow themselves to feel
the presence of this unique, creative, loving energy.*

*I can be nurturing and healing to those who respect
my divine sacred ways.*

*For those of you who come to visit my island and do
not respect my ways, I will shake up your energy to get
your attention. Or I will send you home to not return
again to the island if you don't get the message.*

*My spirit is like lava: flowing fiery red hot but moving
swiftly if need be, or having a steady warming flow*

if that is needed. I work with Mother Earth creating harmony with the tides and the land.

If you need assistance with your relationships, or to find passion for life, call on me to surround you with my fiery energy and create an increased vibration within the feminine ebb and flow within your physical and spiritual body. I will ignite the passion within your sacral and root charkas. Like the color of lava, I will clear your two lower chakras from any past lifetime fears or karma.

If you need assistance connecting with your true passion, ask me for help with this.

If you are in a marriage that needs that little spark you had when you were on your honeymoon, just ask me to ignite a little passion in your relationships and then listen to the clues I give you.

You may wish to visualize your sacral chakra with a beautiful orange-red flame burning gently and then see your orange flame reaching out of your body and asking your partner's or spouse's higher self for permission to connect with his or her sacral passion flame. When you hear confirmation of an affirmative, then see your sacral flame reaching out and uniting with your partner to create a larger flame of a violet color. You will feel this dynamic sexual union, which is connected on an etheric level and will vibrate at a very high dimension. If this feels uncomfortable at first, the flame may have to have a gentler burn. Then you can see the larger flame burning more brightly and larger if you wish to increase the passion between the two of you. This is a sacred method and is to be honored and respected by you.

I wanted to share with you this information, which I have done for many years now and can feel the shift when I wear different-colored underwear. If you wear red or orange underwear, it will tone your sacral and root chakras and you will feel sensual. A good website that has silk chakra underwear is <u>www.marygreen.com</u>. You can order a set of seven pairs of silk chakra underwear that is color-coded to support the seven chakras in your physical body. To keep our chakras running efficiently, we need to support and cleanse them with divine tools on the physical and spiritual levels.

We, as women, need to honor our feminine divine passions and not to be afraid of them. We need to balance the feminine with masculine and this will create harmony. If we have too much fire there is too much heat, so we need to balance the fire with some water. This will keep our root and sacral chakras in balance, which will in turn keep our lives in balance.

One way to do this is to find your true passion, something you love to do, and then do it in balance. There is too much stress in women's lives today, and there are too many expectations to have a great career, have an amazing family, be a chef for your family, exercise, and bake homemade bread. There is a way to have it all and keep the balance in your life; all you need to do is ask for harmony and it will be created.

I will help give you little reminders to slow down and to meditate if you need to or if you're being excessive with one area of your life. If you need to have a fire started underneath you to get you motivated to finish a project, I can do that also. All I ask is that you respect me and I will respect you.

You can create mountains and fire as I can do. You will be amazed at how I can help you get things done at a very efficient rate and you can feel the passion while doing so.

I wanted Velva Dawn to come to Kona again to finish writing her book and to help heal her so that she can move forward and do the life teachings that she needs to do for other women in this lifetime. She kept feeling me pulling her energy to the island until she came back again for the ninth time in twenty-four months. I would really like to have you live here one day when you feel the time is right, Velva Dawn, or you can choose to be a sister anchor for me at another spot around the world too. You will know when the time is right.

Exercise to Ignite Your Sacral Chakra

Here is a healing session that you can use to ignite and maintain the passion in your life. If you don't have the crystals for this exercise, then you can energetically ask them to assist with this exercise. I want you to use a red opal on your root chakra and an orange jasper on your sacral chakra. Light a red candle and an orange candle and place them in your sacred space while doing this healing exercise. Now this session is best if you can sit with your legs in a lotus or cross-legged position with your spine vertical.

Please begin by visualizing yourself like a volcano, your head being the opening of the volcano and your root being the base connected to Mother Earth. Then please place a black obsidian in each hand and gently close your eyes. Slow down your breathing and you may wish to set the intention out to the universe that you wish to ignite your passion within relationships and even to clear those bottom two chakras. Now please open up your crown chakra to the divine and see your roots growing down into Mother Earth and connecting with the hot red lava that is flowing at the base of a volcano. Feel the red lava swirling around your root chakra, slowly but steadily building up pressure ready to erupt. Feel the energy moving in a clockwise rotation.

Then, as you take a deep inhalation, you may feel the lava starting to flow up to the root chakra. See the thick red/orange liquid swirling around in your root and clearing it of any fears you might have in this lifetime and past lifetimes. See this swirling and clearing until the chakra is about the size of a large tomato.

Then feel the lava slowly and gently moving up to the sacral chakra. See the liquid turning a bright orange color, once again moving in a clockwise position clearing and toning this chakra. Take another large inhalation and see the lava-like syrup moving up into the solar plexus chakra, filling it up with passion and power. See the lava melting away any cords of fear that you might have had about anything in life. See the cords melting away and a golden light healing the areas where the cords were attached to any part of your physical body and to heal those people to whom the cords were attached to on their physical body.

Take another deep breath and see the lava in a green color flowing through the heart chakra and filling it with divine love from Mother Earth and Pele. You may feel the lava connecting with your very spirit of who you truly are and what you're truly meant to do in this lifetime. It can be something very gentle and strong or it could be something done with a lot of creativity, passion, and strength. Always know that Pele is with you, giving you strength when you need it. Then feel the lava going through the throat chakra, clearing it of all past issues that you have pent up not saying. Next see it moving up into the third-eye chakra clearing and melting away all fears, allowing you to feel the confidence that you are safe to speak your truth and to share your infinite knowledge in this lifetime.

Finally feel the lava gently erupting out of the top of your crown chakra and flow around your hair and auric field, clearing all of your energy bodies at the same time. Now you may feel the lava flowing all the way from your root, sacral, solar plexus, heart, throat, and third eye and then bursting out of the crown surrounding your personal space. You are now clear and ready to start feeling passion in your relationships, your career, and your family, friends, and hobbies. You may wish to thank Pele for her assistance with this healing, and honor and respect her wisdom.

Remember that you too can have this passion and have balance all wrapped up in one physical body. Take the time to honor your physical, spiritual, mental, and etheric bodies and keep the energy flowing so you don't erupt like Pele. Ebb and flow, fire and water—it's all in the balance of life.

Crystal Healing

You may wish to place the divine fire andara or cuprite on your sacral chakra and/or root chakra. The cuprite crystal represents female power and the red color of both the lava rock and the cuprite represent the blood of Mother Earth and her vital energy.

The vibration at which the cuprite resonates is with the Earth and the moon, which will regenerate and stimulate our healing abilities. Both of these crystals will reconnect us with the primal life force of our root chakras. Before placing either one of these healing crystals on your sacral or root chakra, hold it in your left hand and think of the loving intention that you are wishing to accomplish and what energies you might need assistance with to ground your idea into action.

Affirmation

"Don't be afraid of the fire within. Balance the energy with water and use the fire cycle to move forth working on those projects that you manifest in the water cycles."

Dedication

I would like to dedicate this chapter to my friend Tannis Lee Keeley who embraces her passion and life!

Chapter 5

Luna

Awakening & Revelation

Color: Silver
Crystal: Rainbow Moonstone

I am the sister goddess of the moon shining brightly into the night wearing a silver flowing gown shedding light on those who need transformation and complete healing.

Luna is the sister of the night, waxing and waning from a crescent to a full, round moon. She works with Mother Earth watching over all beings of creation. She closely works with Sister Soleil to keep the relationships of the other goddesses working in harmony to achieve the perfect state of balance in the world.

Luna asks that you bathe in her light when you need healing. She says that the most powerful healing night is the night before the full moon. Go outside and lie beneath the full light near or around white flowers that will reflect her beauty and healing essence.

For women, she is a healing modality that we can use to clear our chakras and to fill them up with pure silver feminine light of the highest vibration. We, as women, are very closely linked with the rhythm of Luna. Our bodies are waxing and waning along with Luna's monthly cycles; this is why it's important to work with her in harmony and not against her.

I can now feel when the full moon is coming. At first I wasn't aware of how Luna's energy affected my body. I would become very irritable about three to four days before the full moon. Then I finally noticed a pattern and asked that my relationship with Luna be in loving harmony with her cycles and that at the rise of the full moon that my energy flow be in rhythm with hers, and that the excess energy be used for love and light to accomplish more projects than I would normally during those times. She answered my prayer and the next month I could feel the harmonious shift, and it was nothing like the volatile month before. I have such high energy when connected to her during that time of the month. It is amazing!

A Gift from Sister Luna

Almost two years ago, we bought a horse named Man Horse from a Native American lady. They called her this because she was never able to carry a foal for them. She was white and beautiful and had a magical spirit so we called her Pegasus.

Months later we noticed that her belly was getting bigger, so we called the veterinarian to come out to confirm if Pegasus was pregnant and, if so, when this foal would come along. Sure enough, he said that she would foal within approximately three months. The excitement in our household was palpable; my girls had always wanted a foal on the ranch! Time could not move fast enough for my daughters.

On August 20, 2007, when we were on a family holiday in Idaho, we got the phone call from my father-in-law who said that there was a new black foal with a white crescent shape on his forehead. Luckily we were heading home already, as the suspense to meet this new little soul was very hard on my girls! We had never had a foal on our cattle ranch before so this would be a first for all of us.

There he was: long spindly legs, beautiful eyes, a shiny black coat of hair and, yes, a white crescent moon in the center of his forehead. He was perfect. I intuitively knew that he had been my horse in a past life and he was a gift from Sister Luna.

The girls enjoyed visiting with Luna and Pegasus daily. Then, on August 30, 2007, on the girls' first day of school, my father-in-law phoned us at home and said that Luna didn't look very good, that he was lying down and looked very weak. So we immediately called our local veterinarian to come as soon as he could.

Every year the school has a pancake breakfast to welcome the kids and staff back to school, so my husband and I were driving down the laneway. We thought that we had time to go into the school for a bit before the vet arrived. We had to drive by Luna and Pegasus's field on the way to the school. As we were driving by them, I could feel my energetic field connect to Luna.

I felt this divine knowing that I needed to go down to where Luna was lying in the field and to start running divine energy into him. This clairsentient feeling was so strong that I literally opened the door of the car as we were slowly driving by. My husband said, "What are you doing?" I firmly told him that I was not going to the school as I needed here with Luna, and he then said to me, "What are you going to do? You're not a veterinarian." I was angry at his response but knew that I must stay. I could hear Luna calling me for help!

As I walked through the green grass to get to Luna, he was barely standing. He was very weak and his eyes were closing. I went up to him and asked god, the angels, the goddesses, and fairies to please help me heal baby Luna. As I started to run the energy into his frail body, he fell onto the green grass. I sat beside him, praying and running energy into him, calling in all beings of love and light.

When our local vet arrived, he said, "I am not sure what his diagnosis is, but usually when we see a horse go down they don't usually survive, but you should take him to another local vet that specializes in equine care." Well there was no option in my mind, so we hooked up the horse trailer and walked Pegasus in and then carefully carried Luna in and laid him down on the straw.

We decided to stop at the school and pick up our girls and asked them to come with us to the vet clinic. We arrived at the veterinary hospital within thirty-five minutes and the vet asked us to back the trailer into their holding area so they could examine Luna. Their diagnosis wasn't good either. They told us the same thing that our local vet had told us, that when a horse goes down it usually doesn't get back up again and survive. So we had two choices: leave him there and they would administer some antibiotics, hydrate him, and monitor him for twenty-four to forty-eight hours, which would be very expensive as it is intensive care, or we could take him home to live what time he had left.

Well there was only one option for us. We all felt such a strong connection to this horse that was just over a week old. I knew that Luna was my horse in a past life.

Our girls were giving Luna kisses on his nose, and as the vet was watching, she said, "Oh, I think that we need to try to save him." And we all unanimously agreed that, yes, we needed to use all life-saving measures for this gift of life. I had a very strong feeling that Luna would survive, despite all of the vets' previous diagnoses.

I was intuitively guided to call Twila Hayes, an energy medicine practitioner who specializes in equine healing. She did a reading on Luna and said that he would survive. She did some healing work on him during our phone call and told me that Luna was grateful for my healing energy and had saved his life. He came to the Earth this time to help me believe in my healing abilities.

During Luna's time at the vet clinic, I put a photo of him on my altar with a rose quartz crystal for healing on top of the photo. I also phoned my close friends Fawna and Leah, who do healing energy work, to please send Luna healing light and to envision him perfectly healed. Then I intuitively received the message that the three of us needed to amplify our healing energy and send Luna healing long distance and also we needed to go and treat Pegasus and Luna together at the vet hospital. I was thinking, *Okay, I am pretty sure the vets aren't going to be open to this but we need to pursue it.* So Fawna, Leah, and I went to the vet clinic, and I said we were there to do some healing work on Luna. The vet said, "What kind of healing work?" I commented, "Well, it's like reiki." She said, "Okay." The vet had told us that during the night Luna had actually gotten up and was walking in circles around the pen and they couldn't believe their eyes! We all smiled and knew that the distance healing energy had made a huge difference in his life.

When we arrived, the vet and her assistant had Pegasus in a stall and they were trying to get Luna to suck to get some milk for him. She told us that when animals are sick, and when the baby has been ill and if the mother feels that her baby is terminal, then the mother/foal bond can be broken. Fawna immediately put her hand at Pegasus's heart center. Leah and I had a hold of Luna and were running energy into him, visualizing the cord between Pegasus and Luna gold and vibrant, and full of love.

Then, within a few tries, Luna latched onto Pegasus's udder and began suckling. The vet looked at us and said, "Oh, my it's a miracle. What did you guys do?" We once again smiled and nodded, saying, "Yes, it's a miracle."

Within forty-eight hours the blood tests results were back so we went to consult with the vet. She said that the blood tests for the West Nile Virus were negative, which is what they thought he originally had, and nothing else was showing up in the results. She thought he might have had an infection in his blood from a source unknown. She also told us that he was walking with his head tilted to the right side and walking in circles to the right, and that he was sensitive to loud noises and that this would never go away! I thought, *Well that's a great sign that he is running in a clockwise direction, which is a healthy flow for energy to move.* I knew that as soon as we got him out of the vet clinic, away from the heavy energy in the building from all of the animals that had died there before him, that he would be perfectly fine.

After five days, the vets were ready to discharge Luna. We loaded him and took him home to be with Pegasus in their own little pen to heal at Chinook Ranch. Sure enough, as soon as we opened the horse trailer door Luna jumped out and ran to greet his mom. He held his head up straight and there was no evidence of him tilting his head. He didn't run in a circle to the right, nor was he sensitive to loud sounds ever again. He was perfect and a miracle had happened here with the help of many divine sources, and of course the sister goddess Luna stepped in and helped out little Luna.

Today Luna is a very loving colt full of divine spirit! The girls can't wait until he is a little older so they can ride him. Deep down, I know that my friend was reconnected with us for a reason.

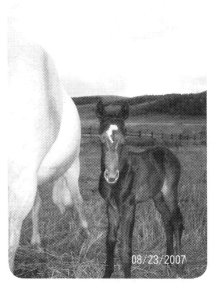

Luna 3 days old   Luna 3 years old

I wanted to tell Luna's story as the moon has very miraculous healing energies and we need to remember to use them in ways for love and light. So next time there is a full moon, go out and put your crystals under the moonlight to cleanse them and then allow your physical body to absorb the energy of sister Luna. You will feel her magical healing!

Crystal Healing

You may wish to place your rainbow moonstone crystal outside during the full moon to cleanse and recharge it for a few days. Then you may wish to place the rainbow moonstone on your heart chakra to help align your energies with the goddess and to empower the feminine aspects of yourself. When connected to your feminine aspect/goddess connection, you will be able to commune with the energies and spirits of Nature, from plant devas to galactic consciousness.

Affirmation

"I am ready to connect to the feminine aspect of myself and to align my goddess energies. Nothing is impossible. I am a whole miraculous being of loving energy. I remember what I am truly here for."

Dedication

I would like to dedicate this chapter to Twila Hayes, an amazing animal healer and intuitive . . . I will always be grateful to you!

Chapter 6

———— ༄ঞ৵৹ ————

Aine

Joy

Color: Green & Purple
Crystal: Purple or Multicolored Fluorite,
or Staurolite

Aine is the goddess of joy. She is also known as the queen mother to the fairies in the elemental realm. She oversees that things are done in an organized manner with joy from the heart center.

Aine worked her magic by leading and showing the fairies lessons in life, including to have fun while doing their daily chores or throwing parties. The fairies love to have parties with their elemental friends, dancing, singing, and eating good food.

This goddess, Aine, is here to teach us ways to have fun in our lives, everything from grounding tasks like taking out the garbage, folding laundry, buying groceries, and setting the table for meals to planning a huge party for all of your friends and other joyous celebrations.

When you wake each morning and you want to have a little extra fun in your day, invoke Aine. Ask her to help you liven up your daily activities. She is very good at giving you good little ideas to keep the day fresh and alive.

This goddess inspired me to start a tradition to have an annual party with about twenty of my closest friends with a theme at my home. The first year was a Japanese theme so I mailed out all of the invitations in handmade origami take-out boxes and had the invitations rolled up, tied with raffia, and attached with an inspirational saying, such as "friendship" on a metal charm inside the box. There was also a pair of chopsticks tied to the top of the box. I asked each of my friends to wear a Japanese-style shirt in a bright color. The party started off with appetizers and cocktails at 5:00 p.m. I could feel the excitement and joy in the air as the women arrived, one by one or two by two, through my front door. I had energetically gridded our front door by asking Mother Mary to stand there while the guests arrived, to allow each woman's heart chakra to be filled with love. I had also invited Archangel Michael and Artemis to stand on our porch, clearing everyone's auric field and making sure that no earthbound spirits or lower energies entered our home.

I was intuitively guided by the angels and archangels to energetically, with loving intention, set up colors along the three-kilometer drive from the highway to my home to tone each chakra of my guests. The first corner started with the root chakra to clear and tone it. The next approach along the road is the sacral chakra driving through an orange color, then moving along through the solar plexus driving through a yellow mist, and halfway up the road intending that each guest would allow her heart center to open wide, clearing lower energies and sending love and assurance with a pink hue. Next was the throat chakra toned with a blue color, and then the third eye with an indigo color and then the crown with a violet ray. Finally, just before driving up to the house, I intended that they drive through a golden light and then a pure white light encompassing all of the colors of the rainbow. I have done this when I have had some relationship issues with certain friends or family members and it has worked divinely. Remember you need to talk to the person with whom you are having an issue to get permission to energetically work on them. If you aren't comfortable speaking to the person, you can always talk to her higher self, asking for permission with loving intent.

This is a good way to keep your home clear of lower and negative energies and to help heal those uncomfortable relationships through miracles. I ask you to try this. You can set it up any way you would like. You can even set up different archangels and/or goddesses along the trip to your home to heal each chakra, or you can even heal different auric layers if need be. These beings of love and light are always around us and wanting to help. We just need to ask them before they can do their divine work.

So when I am planning these parties each year, I do change my guest list depending on what energy I am picking up on each person. I live in a very small community that can be very judgmental and people will talk if they are not invited to an event, but this is when my inner goddess qualities were strongly ignited. I was guided not to worry, dear one you are loved by the divine and it is okay to move forward in life, to connect and surround yourself with higher energies to uplift your soul to a higher connection.

I also invite Aine to be present during events at my home to bring forth a lot of laughter to the celebration and also to help me organize the event from the preplanning of the invitations, shopping for goody bags, decorating my home, cleaning my home, and informing my friends about the event.

Most people who know me know that I love to give goody bags no matter how old they are. I believe that it is fun to get a goody bag from a party; it puts that excitement of not knowing what is in that mystery bag for you. It also awakens the inner child within your soul!

Some years I will tailor each bag for each friend with a thank-you card that I print to match the theme for the party. One year I put all of my favorite things in the bag to celebrate with my friends. I had everything from a chunky Kit Kat to a CD with my favorite songs on it, crystals, and many other girlie fun items.

The meal for my party is prepared by myself and my girlfriends while visiting over a glass of wine and mingling. We have made homemade sushi from scratch, which many of the women had never done before!

When my first friend arrives, I can feel the joy in my heart and her heart. We often feel like an excited child does on the day of his birthday party. I usually have my husband and daughters stay elsewhere so that if the women want to stay up all night and dance and visit that they can sleep over at my home. When women get married and have a family, they rarely take time for themselves, most feeling guilty if they do. So I am on a mission in this lifetime to get women to take care of and celebrate their inner child, and to fill their hearts with joy and love!

Aine is a good role model for all of us! She is very eager and willing to help you organize your day and have it filled with joy while doing those activities that you might not enjoy doing. So before you get out of bed in the morning, invite her to help you throughout the day and to infuse your energy with her essence, uplifting you to help your tasks move along with efficiency and to have fun while doing them. Life is what you make of it, and it can be fun if you allow yourself to enjoy and trust in Aine's energy.

Remember that when we have joy in our hearts and we feed that inner child within each and every one of ourselves that this will indeed have a ripple effect onto our family and friends. We will be better people to be around and can give love from our hearts truly, not begrudgingly. We need to give from a high vibration of wanting to truly give and not give from obligation, which is another whole chapter I will get into later in the book.

Crystal Healing

If you are using the purple or multicolored fluorite, you may wish to lie down and place the crystal at your crown chakra, above your head. This crystal helps you access the higher dimensions of energy while keeping you grounded at the same time. This crystal will enable your decisions to be made with clarity and without hesitation. This crystal will help you walk your talk and be clear about your path if you may have strayed.

If you are intuitively guided to use the staurolite, also known as the fairy stone, you may wish to place this crystal on your third eye assisting you in communicating with the fairy realm. This crystal will also help increase your ability to communicate with animals if you are wishing to do this. You may even place the fluorite at your crown chakra and the staurolite at your root chakra, allowing you access to the higher realms above and the fairy realms at the ground level. Have fun with this healing. It is truly magical.

Affirmation

"I am worthy of having joy in my life and celebrating the carefree and fun energy of the fairies. It is okay to ask Aine to assist me with anything I need in my life to bring about happiness and lift the waves of stress out of my auric field."

Dedication

This chapter is dedicated to my friend Fawna Bews.

Chapter 7

Artemis

Protection

Color: Metallic Black
Crystal: Black Arrowhead Obsidian,
or Orange Carnelian

Artemis is the goddess who carries a bow and arrow at her side, waiting to protect herself and her loved ones. She's a warrior spirit inside and out, ready to defend the ones she loves.

You may call upon her when you are feeling that you need extra protection or shielding from negative and lower energies.

Artemis can help you put up healthy boundaries around yourself. As women, we tend to think that if we say "no" when someone asks us to volunteer at our child's school or to bake a pie for a fundraiser that we are not pulling our weight. We may have a list of twenty things to do that day and not one of them will include *time for me* on their list. A lot of women think that the more they can tick off their list, the better they will feel about themselves. But what they need to realize is that when you don't feed your soul, the heart chakra, you will soon become resentful, bitter, and will be giving from a place of depletion and negative energy that won't be healthy for anyone, including your family. Why is it that we do this to ourselves?

We need to give back to ourselves before *the glass is half empty*. If you can even allow fifteen to twenty minutes a day when you're in the bath or before you jump out of bed in the morning, do a quick meditation or prayer to center yourself and to set your intentions of what *you* need for the day, and ask the goddesses and angels for assistance. They are waiting by our sides just wanting us to ask, but remember they can't take action until we give them our permission.

We need to infuse some of Artemis's qualities into our energy field to allow some balance in our lives and to remain centered in a loving and positive way. Artemis will help you set boundaries for yourself, by loving yourself is first and foremost. She will help you have the courage to say no when you are asked to go to the hundredth home party for your neighbor when you really don't need any more jewelry but don't have the heart to tell her so.

She will guide you to say "no" with light and love. Moving forward in this direction will give you a healthier outlook on life from the physical point of view, decreasing stress in your life, and from the spiritual realm also. We can get stuck in the superwoman role of doing everything for everyone else, but really deep inside our souls we are feeling very tired, lonely, and bitter and we are not loving life at all! You may even be living parts of your life in denial, unable to see these qualities so you are not able to deal with them until you are ready. Then, eventually, your physical body may become ill and you may wonder why.

Maintaining healthy boundaries is a quality that we all can use in this world today. Everyone is so busy with life that they may forget who they are and what they really love to do! You may lose the spark of your inner child, not knowing how to nurture yourself, but you can make one hundred peanut butter sandwiches for the PTA meeting tonight and by the time you get to the meeting you are so zoned out that you don't even hear what is being said. Consequently you pick up tons of negative energy, going to bed exhausted and then starting all over again tomorrow, not looking forward to life.

Does this sound like you? I do know a few of these women, and I was one myself until I started exploring the metaphysical world and seeing the negative effects of not having any healthy boundaries and how this could have an affect your body. It even resulted in death for some whom I knew.

After I had my first daughter Kayla, I quit my job at the hospital where I had worked full-time for over ten years, making my own money, to now be at home as a full-time mother and wife to a rancher, depending on him as my source of income.

Imagine how well that went for me . . . not good! Soon I was depressed, overweight, tired, and resentful. What happened to the perfect mom myth, that once I had a baby everything would be perfect? Well, this is how the hamster wheel begins, ladies. You want to be the perfect wife, cooking and cleaning for your husband when you're married, and then having a baby and adding that to your routine of giving.

After having two more daughters, Josie and Erin, I started to figure it out. What time was I giving to myself and why did I feel guilty when I thought I might need some time to be alone? Why do we place this feeling of guilt on ourselves for thinking that we deserve some quality alone time?

Guilt is one of the lowest vibrations that we can carry around, so now I can tell you that as soon as I feel this lower vibration, which can be felt as a heaviness in your heart or solar plexus chakra, I acknowledge it and then release it. There is no need to carry it around and feel sick from it. I have learned to ask that those negative emotions be lifted out of my auric field by all divine beings. The more often you take a little time for yourself, the easier it is not to feel guilty. Your spiritual self will begin to crave this reflective time; it is needed to remain healthy.

Artemis can help protect you and your family. She may teach you the need for healthy lifestyle maintenance of having some quality time getting to know your higher self. You will be a better person, a better wife, a better mother, daughter, sister, and friend to all of those who know you when you honor yourself, so will others. You will radiate a positive, loving, balanced energy from your auric field and this will have a very healthy effect on your children. They will see that when their mother takes time for herself that she is more content and loving toward the entire family. You are being a good role model for your children when you maintain healthy boundaries.

The generations who worked from sunrise to sunset are long gone, my friends. We are the new generation living a healthy, centered, loving, and harmonious life with passion and peace. We realize that we need to do yoga or some form of physical movement daily to release the blocks within our chakras that will prevent disease from entering our auric field.

Artemis asks that when you need her for protection, or to assist with personal boundaries, please ask her to stand by your side and to allow you to feel her strength and to give you the voice of reason to say "no" when you need to in a loving way that everyone involved will understand.

She is a warrior and wants to revive some of that energy within each and every one of you.

When you need her call on her, she will be there by your side gently but firmly guiding you to set healthy boundaries for yourself until you see that you can do it by yourself. You too have the qualities of a very strong warrior goddess, brave enough to do the toughest things in life while standing tall with your arrow in your hand, if need be, protecting your inner child along with your family. Move forward in life bravely and lovingly and all things that are meant to be will fall into place, dear goddess!

Crystal Healing

Black obsidian shaped in an arrowhead will act as a protective barrier around your auric field or your home if you wish. If you would like to protect your home from any negative energies, you may wish to place this crystal on the left side or center of your doorway. For your own personal healing, you may wish to place the obsidian crystal at your root chakra during meditation to give you the real insight as to what it is that you have been hiding in the shadows in your life and haven't been wanting to deal with. This crystal will help you bring those qualities forth and heal when the timing is right.

In addition to the obsidian, place the orange carnelian crystal on your sacral or solar plexus chakra. This crystal will help you take the action you need to create your perfect reality. Never look at life as being a failure. Remember that each action leads to an experience and each experience adds wisdom to your reality that you can share with others, ultimately leading you to your goal of self-understanding.

Affirmation

"I will honor my needs first, viewing my body as my temple and filling it up with high vibrating affirmations, friendships, healthy boundaries, and loving movement."

Dedication

I would like to dedicate this chapter to my sister goddess friend Tatiana Scavnicky, who honors her boundaries.

Chapter 8

―――∘᪥⁂᪥∘―――

Brigit
Self-Dignity

Color: Light Green
Crystal: Blue Lace Agate

Brigit is a Celtic goddess from Ireland representing the three parts of a woman's life: the young virgin, the loving mother, and the wise woman (the crone). She is often depicted having long red hair and piercing blue eyes and standing in her own energy. She is also known to protect whoever asks for her help.

Stand firmly in your own soil, the gift of Mother Earth, knowing that you can speak your inner truth, be heard, and be honored. You are safe during this time to honor your feminine sacred self and allow your true words of wisdom be sowed when needed

I was a warrior in my days, fighting like a man on my horse with my sword in my hand. My thoughts are like fire: ignited easily and burning steadily, allowing the passion to develop within.

I know that many women have an intense heat within their physical, spiritual, mental, and etheric bodies, and they think that it is bad to feel such intensity within their own bodies, let alone their own lives.

Heat/fire is a good element to carry within. You need to learn balance within the fire, which allows time for cleansing and nurturing along with the cycles of rapid productive work.

There will be cycles in my life, being an Aries, when I will be able to accomplish huge tasks in a matter of hours. This is not comprehensible to others.

One morning, I recall getting up, having my breakfast and my morning cup of Kona coffee, and I decided to sit down at my computer and design my own website for my business. I finished within five hours

After that, I painted the bathroom walls a different color and decided to change all of the electrical décor from brass to silver. When this happend, my husband said, "What are you doing? You are still in your pajamas."

These are the fire cycles, the most efficient productive cycles in my days/weeks/months. I honor these cycles now and, yes, they usually correspond with the full moon cycle.

I know that I can portray some of the qualities of superwoman during these days and I also know that this will slow down with Mother Earth's rhythms, and the time for me to nurture myself and go into a cocoon is all a healthy balance.

Many people have said to me, "How do you get so much done, having three children, a husband, living on a ranch, being part of a community, and running your own business?"

I now know that it is tapping into that divine fire energy and allowing it to flow through my chakras to assist me with my daily activities no matter how little or small they are. I start each morning holding my hands up to the moon, the sun, and universal infinite energies of divine love and light connecting my chakras and auric field to these limitless energies. I can feel the surging of this energy in my physical being and then allowing my auric field to expand to an unlimited field connecting to these expansive divine energies. Breathing deeply, I can allow this silver and gold energy frequency to increase the vibration of my intuition and to allow my physical energy to be amplified. I ask you to try this exercise while grounding your roots into Mother Earth, feeling the energy surging throughout your chakras connecting to the true divine source.

Take the time each day to ask Brigit to help you wash your floors or to help you be the volunteer mom during your child's special day at school, or to help get the fire started underneath you to get your physical body moving.

Sometimes we forget that we aren't alone in this world and that we have our special team of divine helpers who will assist us in whatever we need during any moment in time.

When the fire cycles are complete, and I am finished being superwoman, I will then have these days when I need to nurture my soul every day.

One of the ways that I will do this is to take extra time meditating during these cycles, knowing that my spiritual and physical bodies are transforming and that I need to take extra time to focus, sending love to my body. I will meditate on my amethyst biomat with a gridding of crystals that I am guided to use from the goddesses for that specific session. I light some candles and invoke god, archangels, angels, goddesses, and all beings of love and light to allow me to transform and to heal whatever it is that my body specifically needs at that time.

I will book myself a massage with a therapist who has good energy about him or her, or I will book a pedicure for myself. I will go outside and lie on Mother Earth, allowing the sunshine to gently warm my face and body, cleansing and nurturing my soul from all of the hard work that I have accomplished in my fire cycle.

At first, I thought that maybe I was suffering from depression, but now I know that I am an Aries superwoman, wise woman, mother, author, teacher, friend, and wife. I need to honor all of the cycles in my life that I will go through.

In fact, at one point, when my husband and I were having some marital issues, as we all go through, my family physician recommended that I go see a psychologist and look for some help.

I have seen many women around me prescribed antidepressants for their emotional struggles in life, and I have always had a feeling that this would not be a good choice for me.

A few weeks into our counseling sessions, the doctor recommended that I try a week's worth of antidepressants to see if it would help. When I look back I can see that the reality of this situation was that I was in a fire cycle and I didn't know how to contain my fiery energy so my temper would flare. I now know that I am a wise one and we tend to know things are going to happen before they do. I have had to learn not to judge others for not having this wisdom.

The doctor broke me down during this session with her authoritative energy, and asked that I try these pills for seven days. I could hear Brigit saying, "Don't take those pills. I can give you the knowledge that you need to harmonize the fire energy within your soul. You are an amazing sister who has cycles of fire and water, and all you need are the ancient tools to help you flow through these cycles of nature. You were given these divine qualities to help empower others in your lifetime. Please trust in me and download this knowledge to share with others, so that they too can be medication free."

But that night I took just one tiny white pill, and within a few hours my head was spinning out of control, my pulse was racing, and I was positive that my throat was closing off and I was going to die. So I phoned the health link to talk with a nurse to see if I was in fact going to die. She informed me that my pulse was normal and that I would be okay. I must also add that she became very impatient with my questions and firmly told me not to worry. I was shown a glimpse of how people who suffer with mental illness may not always be treated with respect.

I had to sit upright in the bathtub most of the night so that I could breath. Needless to say, I will never forget that night as long as I live.

The next morning I flushed the last six pills down the toilet and was angry with myself for allowing another woman to beat my spirit down and to try to solve my high energy by medicating me with drugs. The doctor never called me to see how I was doing with my new medication, as I strongly sent her the message that I no longer wished to have a connection with her at all. I could feel my auric field expand and strengthen from this moment.

When I saw my family physician at a later date, she asked me how the counseling was going. I told her that the psychologist had tried to put me on antidepressants and that I flushed them down the toilet. She said that she didn't think that I needed to be on medication in the first place and was shocked that the psychologist had prescribed them to me. I replied, "Yes I know." I think that too many doctors are overprescribing antidepressants so that people are numb!

We are entering a very high vibrating energy change on planet Earth and I know that I want to be awake and ready to move forward with these changes, feeling everything along the way: good or bad. With the divine's help, all is possible.

I am in no way saying that I disagree with the use of antidepressants, but I do feel that they are very much overprescribed.

I thank Brigit for giving me the strength to say "no" to an authority figure. I am grateful that she was there to help guide me and give me the courage to step forward into my own power and know that I can handle my fiery energy in a natural way using all divine beings of love and light.

So I ask you to call upon Brigit the Celtic goddess to hold your hand along your path when you are wavering. She is there if you ask her to be.

You may even wish to invoke her when you are lighting a candle during meditation or on your altar to symbolize her fire!

Crystal Healing

Please place the blue lace agate on your throat chakra to assist in communication with your higher self and teach us that our words create our reality. You may also wish to place this crystal on your third-eye chakra to calm an overstimulated mind and soothe your thoughts during meditation. The blue lace agate will help you to express your true thoughts and to overcome the fear of judgment of others and your own self-doubt. You may also use this crystal to calm the fire energy in your throat chakra to help harmonize your emotions.

Affirmation

"I am lovingly able express my innermost thoughts to all without fear of judgment and self-doubt. My inner voice is honored with love and light sharing my wisdom with others who may learn from my words. My communication vibrates from the highest level of love and light. I am whole."

Dedication

I would like to dedicate this to my friend Karen Snodgrass who trusted the divine and allowed herself to be free.

Chapter 9

―――∘〰∞〰∘―――

Sedna

Infinite Supply

Color: Sea foam Green
Crystal: Green Fluorite

*I am the goddess of the sea supplying abundance for
all sea creatures, flowing with the ebb and flow of the
ocean's tides, swimming freely with all of my ocean
friends.*

Sedna's message to all of her fellow goddesses is to know that
no matter what we choose in life, if we are truly following our
life path with love and light then we will be supplied in all ways.
It is our fear that creates the blocks within our chakras that
keep us from receiving what we have prayed for and wanted.
We don't realize sometimes that we can sabotage ourselves by
letting our egos creep in and allow fear to build up in our mind
and body.

We do have control over our thoughts. We need to first of
all be aware of them when they occur and then acknowledge
them, thank them, and then release them for the good, sending
them to Mother Earth to be recycled into love and light for all
of the world to benefit.

Sedna says that centuries ago people's needs weren't so
materialistic. They had the basic needs met—water, food,
shelter, and love—and we need to get back to having those
most important basic needs met in life. We need to remember to

fill our bodies with pure, highly energized water daily, drinking one to two liters per day. A good way to purify and amplify the healing ability within your drinking water is to envision white light transmuting and swirling around in your glass before every sip and seeing the white light infusing and healing all areas of your body. It is also very important to swim in ocean water to purify your auric field and clear it from any negative or lower energy, and to also cleanse your physical body.

Go for a swim with the sea animals and heal yourself from toxicity. If it is not possible for you to go for a swim in the ocean, then you can have a warm bath and put two to four tablespoons of Dead Sea salt in the water and try to remain in the bath for fifteen to twenty minutes to allow the water to cleanse your physical body and clear your aura (make sure it is Dead Sea salt if possible, as it has the highest mineral content and draws toxins out of your physical body).

Sedna suggests that we need to nourish our bodies with good organic foods: fruits, vegetables, and organic meat if you are not a vegetarian or vegan. She says that some people's bodies do need the protein, so check with your higher self and see what your body needs. You can also do this by muscle-testing yourself or by using the body pendulum test: allowing your body to be the pendulum itself, going forward three times before you hold the food and saying this way is "yes" and then leaning backward and this direction means "no." Please make sure that your feet are firmly grounded before doing this test. Next, hold the food that you are wondering about in your hand and ask your body if this food is good for your body. You will get a response of "yes" moving forward or "no" leaning backward. Trust that this is your answer. You can also use this method when eliminating foods from your diet if you are having allergies, and also you can use this method of testing your body when deciding what vitamins and minerals it may need.

Sedna is urging us to make sure to find our food sources from a high-energy market or farm that is organic. Check out the staff in the store and see how their energy feels to you; if you don't get a good feeling in the store then go elsewhere. It's okay to make changes in your life. The goddesses will support and guide you if you ask them. Sedna is very willing to answer any questions that you might have. Just ask her by saying it in your head, out loud, or by writing her a letter. She will answer you.

Shelter is a basic need that we all have. Sedna is asking if we are building a new home to try to use Earth-friendly building supplies, flooring, window coverings, low-flush toilets, energy-efficient windows and insulation. We need to remember that we have children who are going to be using this planet for a long time after us and we need to make sure that it is healthy for them. We need to keep in mind that we need to make better choices now as they will affect our future and theirs.

When buying a home that was previously owned by someone else or renting an apartment, make sure you check out the energy of the building and the landlord/owner to make sure that their energy is of a high source. Cleanse the area before you move in by asking the goddesses to help you do what the area needs. You could smudge it with sweet grass or sage; you may use crystals in the area and grid it for a time before moving in. You may visualize white light purifying the home and asking Archangel Michael and Artemis to clear the energy. It is important that we clear the energy on a regular basis to keep our homes and humans healthy and happy.

There is always an infinite supply of love to go around the world for everyone. We need to get to the source of where love is for ourselves and then tap into that source and send it to ourselves, our loved ones, our friends, and all those who may need it around the world.

We need to remember that there is an infinite supply of whatever we need if love and light is our main focus. When we remove the worry and fear and get to the center of the source, all will be supplied. We just need to listen and trust.

Sedna's healing tips are to cleanse regularly in the ocean or a bath with Dead Sea salt in it, daily if possible, and to eat only organic foods that will nourish your physical body. Cleanse your area of shelter on a daily or weekly basis, and fill your hearts with the infinite supply of love everyday and then send the love from your heart out to the planet, the oceans, the forests, Mother Earth, Father Sky, God, and all beings of love and light.

Crystal Healing

You may wish to place the green fluorite upon your heart chakra with the intent of vacuuming out any clutter, negativity, astral confusion, stagnant emotions, old wounds, and clearing the home of your soul. The green crystal will help cleanse and heal the heart chakra and allow the energy to flow in harmony from the heart to the mind, allowing true deep healing to occur on all levels.

Affirmation

"My mind and heart are in harmony with one another, allowing my true life purpose to be fulfilled with passion and harmony. I will heal all of my wounds in this lifetime to remember that I am whole and that I am loved infinitely, receiving blessings of abundance."

Dedication

I would like to dedicate this chapter to my soul sister Katherine Huber.

Chapter 10

Green Tara
Delegation

Color: Emerald Green
Crystal: Green Aventurine or Malachite

Green Tara is a Buddhist and Hindu goddess. Her name represents star in the Sanskrit language. She is the goddess of universal compassion and her name means "she who saves." Green Tara is often depicted in a posture of ease and readiness for action. She is believed to help those following her to overcome dangers, fears, and anxieties, and she is ultimately worshipped for her ability to overcome the most difficult obstacles. She will act quickly when you call upon her.

Green Tara is the goddess that gives us the strength to delegate projects. Many of us in life have trouble saying "no" when people ask us to do things. This can be for your children's school council to bake cookies, to lead a women's group in your community, etc. Once you get married and have children, your personal responsibilities keep increasing. Now you have double the Christmas shopping to do; you had already bought Christmas gifts for your family, but now you somehow become responsible for buying for your husband's side of the family, then filling your own children's stockings and possibly rounding up a food hamper or two for families that are in need in your community! How did this happen? You have now run yourself ragged and are feeling very bitter and resentful, and it's supposed to be a joyous Christmas season! Did you miss something or is this how everyone else is feeling and they just aren't voicing it?

Chances are most women feel empty at some point in their lifetime! We sometimes feel like we are superwoman and that we can multitask, but truly deep down we are void of loving ourselves and standing in our own power saying "no" to others' demands on our time. Balance is the key as with all life lessons. Compassion for yourself should be of the highest priority within your life and daily tasks.

Green Tara is urging you to ask her to help you delegate jobs wherever you need to do this. She will help you develop a chore chart for your children and husband if need be, dividing up the tasks so that everyone's energy remains balanced and healthy. She will help you make lists at work, sharing the projects whether they are big or small. An equal exchange of energy is vital to our health in many ways. Green Tara will help you empower yourself by standing firmly in your big girl or big boy boots, allowing your energy to flow evenly and harmoniously between your chakras.

No one benefits from being superwoman or superman all of the time, nor is it healthy! It's okay to take a leadership role in your life, but this doesn't mean that you have to do everything in your household and at work. You will end up sick if you try to continue living your life in an unbalanced state of energy exchange. Receiving is just as important as giving.

You can manifest people to delegate your tasks to if need be. Remember we create what we think, so if you need an extra pair of hands to help decorate the community hall for a wedding, put that intention out there to the universe that someone will lovingly come along and volunteer to help you with this project. It will happen. You must not have any strings attached as to whom it will be or how they will appear; just send out the positive thought for help and then patiently wait for the answer as it will come!

Green Tara loves to dispense her wisdom with delegation. I have asked Green Tara to help me in delegating chores around my home allowing me time to finish this book that I have been writing for three years now. I have invited her into my life to help me complete a task when I need help to see through to completion.

Green Tara's message to me:

> *Dear sister, I am thankful that you have taken the time to invite me into your life. I have been wanting to help you finish this book and many other projects that you have had on the go for a few years now. You have the ability to make a checklist of what your priorities are, completing them, and then checking them off your list. If you don't organize your thoughts onto paper, you don't know what you're looking at, so take a few minutes each morning to write down goals that you want to accomplish in your life in these areas: personal, spiritual, financial, and physical.*

It is important that you also make some type of movement for your physical body. Exercise is a necessity throughout your day to help ground your ideas from your head into your root chakra so that you have the support of Mother Earth to follow through with your goals and intentions. Many people have millions of ideas floating around in their minds, but unless they move that energy to the root chakra to be supported by our Mother, it is likely that these ideas will remain as energy spinning in our minds unless it is moved down to the red root chakra. Funny, I just realized that I am wearing a red shirt today to support my root chakra!

Please try not to be that superhero and do everything yourself. Ask for Green Tara to help you gain the support and wisdom of your own personal divine team to help you organize and evenly spread out your workload to live a healthy, happy, and harmonious life! It is important to have compassion for your soul, allowing it time to be nurtured and to reflect so that you will have the strength and energy to follow through with the divinely guided ideas that you will receive during or after those moments of stillness.

Green Tara's teachings are about balancing the act of stillness and nurturing with that of action and following through with your thoughts and goals. She asks that you write her a letter telling her about all of your ideas and goals that you are wishing to achieve in this lifetime. You may also wish to tell her that you are willing to put yourself at the top of the list. You will receive answers from her intuitively, by thoughts that cross your mind, or if you like to channel you may wish to sit down and connect with Green Tara with pen in hand and ask to be a divine channel of wisdom for her guidance for you. She can help you work through obstacles that you think are completely impossible to overcome.

Crystal Healing

You may wish to place the green aventurine on your heart chakra to begin the process of opening this center to compassion for yourself and others. Green aventurine will help heal old emotional trauma and patterns that are stored within your physical bodies at a DNA level, which can eventually lead to imbalance and then to disease. Breathe deeply while this crystal is upon your heart center and allow its healing vibrations to open your heart to new levels.

You may also wish to use the green malachite on your solar plexus chakra to help align your will with the divine and the universe. This crystal will help reduce the sound of the ego and the wanting of material possessions in the physical world. You will begin to feel the balance and the right use of your will, resulting in resolutions that are for the highest good of all.

Affirmation

"I can feel the compassion in my soul resulting in universal harmony for the highest good of all beings of love and light. I am ready to make my ideas and goals a priority in my life, asking Green Tara and the divine team to join me in delegating tasks within my life to help me fulfill those divine thoughts."

Dedication

I would like to dedicate this chapter to Joan Blayney who passed away in 2010. She was an amazing teacher and friend to me and I feel very fortunate to have known her.

Chapter 11

———◦⚬✿⚬◦———

White Tara
Sensitivity

Color: Pale Green
Crystal: Clear Quartz or Green Jade

White Tara is on Hindu descent, she is sometimes found representing the female face on a Buddha. White Tara has seven eye symbols on her forehead, hands, and feet representing her intentions or prayers and her ability to see all of the suffering in the world. She is sometimes called the Mother of all Buddhas. She represents the motherly nature and her color is white, representing purity, wisdom, and truth. She is richly adorned with jewels. White Tara sits upon a lotus flower representing the center of your heart chakra. She is associated with being sensitive pertaining to your physical body and to longevity.

The world is full of harsh chemicals, food preservatives, pollution, negative energy, and toxic waste. We need to take the time to strip away all of the lower and harsh energies that surround our auric fields, which inhibit our energy body from functioning at its optimum levels. Consequently our physical bodies don't function adequately. Body functions slow down and eventually sickness may set in. There are so many levels that surround our auric field.

The basic seven layers of the aura are the etheric, the emotional body, the mental body, the astral body, the etheric template, the celestial body, and the ketheric template. Some of you will take lifetimes to work through the lower energies that you carry from past lives.

Many of you are here on the planet this time for the celebration that will be coming with the planetary shift that is already occurring. You may have chosen to come and enjoy this life with Mother Earth and her sisters. The divine feminine is awakening from centuries of lying stable within the core, waiting for her female and male counterparts to gain the knowledge and wisdom that they need to help harmonize this shift. Many of you already know that you are one of those warriors; some of you have already stepped out and have begun your careers as healers and professional speakers. I congratulate you for showing this strength and stepping forward.

Along the path, you need to shed those layers of past lifetime fears and deaths, allowing you to fully step into the wise soul that you truly are. There have been and continues to be many transformations that you will go through physically, mentally, and spiritually until you are ready to live your spiritual authentic life.

Are you honest when others ask what you do for a living? When your family members don't have the same spiritual beliefs that you do? This can be very hard and intimidating when you feel like you are a spiritual warrior. If you grow up in a family that doesn't use their intuition as their main source for decision making, this can be confusing to those who do have a very strong intuitive side and aren't encouraged to use it.

As a child, I had very bad eczema on my inner arms, behind my knees, and behind my ear lobes. The eczema was so bad on my inner arms that I would scratch it until it bled and then it would sting when I had to have a bath. A special time that I remember as a child was nighttime. I used to have my dad rub the salve on my inner arms to help with the inflammation. I remember praying to God every night, asking to please take away this painful eczema on my body.

I remember when I was in grade one and started school. One of the children in my class asked me what was wrong with my arms and why it looked like I had raspberry jam smeared on my inner arms. I used to hide my arms by wearing long sleeves all of the time, whether it was warm or cold.

I grew up in Alberta, Canada, where we have snow in the wintertime. We would have families gather on a neighbor's land and we would toboggan down the hills and visit with the neighbors. I loved this annual event, except for one very awkward part of myself that made me very self-conscious: my eczema. When I had the salve on my arms, my mom would then put plastic wrap around my arms so that the salve would soak into my skin rather than onto my clothing.

When I would move my arms, you could hear the crinkling from the plastic wrap and people would ask me what the noise was. Many times these thoughts would stop me from wanting to go out into public places.

I am proud to say that by the age of thirteen I outgrew the eczema. I learned that I was very sensitive to many different foods. I also say that the divine had a major role in healing my eczema and that the eczema was a symptom that I was very sensitive to many things in my surroundings, which affected me on all levels.

White Tara is the goddess that you may call upon to help you become aware of foods that your body can't digest or may be sensitive to. Just ask her to help you eliminate those toxic foods from your diet and she will show you how. When you are shopping for groceries, ask White Tara to accompany you and you can move the energy within your body to show you which foods are good for you and which aren't. You may do this by moving the energy in a way that you can feel it. You may ask your body to amplify the energy in your solar plexus (belly area) as a "yes" if the food choices will assist you in holding divine energy. Then ask that your energy be amplified in your heart chakra if the food will not be supportive to you holding divine energy. You may move the energy around any way you feel is good for you. To be aware and listen to your body is the key to living a healthy fulfilling life. When your body has an inflammation of any type in any area, you need to get to the source of this rather than just treating the symptoms. When I look back at my childhood eczema, I know that those chakras in my elbows, knees, and behind my ears, though they may be minor chakras, needed to be cleared. At that time, I didn't know how to do this. Oprah says, "We do better when we know better," and that is an amazing quote to live by.

Listen to your body! I am now forty years old and feel like I have finally shed many of those layers of lower energy that were surrounding my auric field through the assistance of healers, reiki, crystals, elixirs, meditations, goddesses, god, and love! Mostly I learned to love myself for who I truly am and honor what I authentically feel.

When I reflect on my childhood, I can see many times when my body was telling me that I was a sensitive soul and tried to alert me to listen to it!

Being in an environment of negative energy and polluting your body with processed foods, sugars, and artificial ingredients takes a toll on your body in many ways. Few of us figure out how to eliminate the toxins from our bodies and freely move upon our path. Many never figure this out, becoming ill and remaining victims frozen in old ways and fear!

I want to share a little story with you about getting to know White Tara. As I began this chapter in my book, if there is a goddess that I am not as familiar with I will ask her to surround her energy around my field and then invite her energy into my auric field so that I may experience her true essence. During this chapter, I took a break as my girls arrived home from school.

Now please take into account that I was drinking my healing elixirs, making sure that I felt the vibrations of the elixirs before selling them. Within a few hours of inviting White Tara's energy into my energy field, I started to feel very weepy and sad. This sadness then progressed into a full-fledged sobbing straight from heart. I went outside several times to clear the energy and to ground myself to figure out why I was feeling so sad. My husband asked me what was wrong. He asked me if it was that time of the month for me. I said, "I don't know what is wrong. I feel very sad and I can't stop crying." I even spent a few minutes sobbing while sitting in the bathroom, as I knew that my emotions were as upsetting to everyone around me as they were to me. Finally, after a day of these emotions, I was on the phone with my friend Kathy and I was telling her that I couldn't stop crying and that I didn't know why I was feeling this way.

Kathy is a very dear friend of mine, and very intuitive herself, and she said, "Did you tap into why you're feeling this way?" Bing! Light-bulb moment for me. I said, "Thank you. You just helped me figure out why I am feeling this way."

I just realized that I had intentionally asked White Tara to surround me with her energy and then I drank a few bottles of my healing goddess elixirs. I then meditated using eight different andara crystals on my chakras. This could be why I was feeling so sensitive and emotional. White Tara's energy is about feeling sensitive. The healing elixirs cleared my chakras and the andara crystals amplified all of this!

Many of my friends laugh at me, saying that I always have to do things in a big way. I had just done so again. Having a scientific background, I always need to prove things to myself by feeling them to know that they actually do work, and I usually ask for it to be amplified so I know this for sure!

I have since learned to trust and to ask that my lessons have a more graceful and harmonious answer to them. I now know that I can learn in a gentle way and it will still be as powerful.

All in all, White Tara is wishing to help you, loving you, and waiting to help you clear whatever it is that you feel that you need to clear.

Crystal Healing

You may wish to use the clear quartz crystal on any of your chakras for transmutation and clarity. You may also place this crystal above your head at your crown chakra with the intention that it will clear all of the other chakras in your body. The clear quartz can energize, balance, and clear all of your chakras. You may wish to call upon the energies of the clear quartz and White Tara to assist you in becoming clear about the choices that lie ahead of you. You may also ask that this crystal clear the lower energy that may be clogging up your body and auric field, and then assist you in making decisions to choose a healthy vibrant lifestyle.

You may also wish to use green jade crystal upon your heart chakra for healing and well-being. You may instantly feel the positive effects of this crystal when placed upon your heart center. The jade crystal fosters the growth of your chi or life-force energies. Jade helps to stimulate the flow of energy throughout the body and supports the never ending well of abundance that is connected to the universe.

Affirmation

"I am willing to listen to the symptoms that my physical body is telling me to heal. I will nurture my boundaries and dietary needs to help the sensitive part of my soul evolve with love and kindness."

Dedication

I would like to dedicate this chapter to my soul sister and friend Chris Marmes. Thank you for your infinite access to higher realms and knowledge.

Chapter 12

———◦⟊⟊⟊◦———

Kuan Yin
Self-Fulfillment

Color: Purple
Crystal: Rhodonite, Kyanite

Kuan Yin is an Eastern goddess who is the true essence of gentleness, warmth, and compassion for others and how we feel about ourselves. Part of her life path is to stay near Mother Earth to help awaken all souls to the light. She is the goddess who will help you release all judgments about yourself and others. She asks that you look at yourself through the eyes of love at all times and to be gentle on yourself.

> *We need to love our souls to the very core, looking into our souls as the perfect seeds of love and light that god/goddess created within each of us. Please ask me to help you release all judgments that you may have about yourself or others. You may be living in an environment that is very toxic, condemning others for their actions. It is time to let go and release all words describing how others should be in your eyes. It is time to release all preconceived notions of how you yourself should, could, and would be. Please ask me to assist you with this process; be gentle with yourself.*

Kuan Yin asks us to all see our heart chakras like a beautiful pink rose gently opening up one petal at a time to receive love and compassion from others and from ourselves. Many times it is easy for us to have compassion for others and their actions, but if you are like me it is hard to have compassion and feel a sense of peace about your own actions.

I have a tendency to push myself very hard and to be very critical of myself in all things that I do. It has taken me over three years to write this book. I kept telling myself, *Who would want to read this book? I am not an author. What do I think I am doing writing a book?* It has taken a lot of spiritual work and trust in the divine, the goddesses, and myself to move forward to finish this book.

From an early age, I remember being a perfectionist about my schoolwork, having to get an A+ in all of my subjects at school. I wanted to be everyone's friend on the playground, counseling friends at an early age as to what they should do with certain situations in their lives.

I was in the 4-H Beef Club and once a year we had to write a two—to three-minute speech and also do a one—to two-minute impromptu speech. I could feel the butterflies flying around in my stomach, along with the palms of my hands getting hot. I now realize that this feeling was my solar plexus chakra and hand chakras activating to help expand the energy within my power center to flow through my body out of my hands. This expanded my auric field to tap into the divine infinite akashic records. This is a tool that I want to teach all souls to use and recognize within their physical bodies.

When we are about to speak and share our wisdom with others, our crown chakra will open up wide like a lotus flower expanding and opening all of the petals. Then this allows the divine energy to flow down through your head to your third eye and then expand your throat chakra to allow your words to be expressed with light and love. Next your heart expands your speech so it is felt with passion and love. Your solar plexus (power center) is to be charged with this energy giving you the strength and wisdom to stand in front of a group of souls to share your information. This energy will then flow down to your sacral, creative chakra to ad lib if you need to answer any questions that might come up during the presentation. Finally you ground this divine energy into Mother Earth, allowing her to be your anchor/root supporting you through this event. You may feel the divine energy tingling through your body from head to toe, allowing your body to be a channel for divine wisdom to flow through you with purity and love with sharing with others. This is a very good visual to do before you have to get up and speak in front of a group of people in any situation.

I have found this technique very useful when I am teaching a workshop. I used to type up pages of notes to make sure that I didn't forget anything and that I had all of the answers in case anyone asked. Then as I practiced and grew in my spiritual world, my trust in channeling the information from the divine grew and expanded also. I do type up a brief outline of what I am going to present at a workshop and then I ask to be a pure divine channel of information that this specific group needs to hear from me on that day. One of the last times I did a workshop in Edmonton, I was doing the Atlantean Activation and Dolphin Healing Workshop with Athena and I added a few extra sentences into my previously recorded "Igniting the Goddess Flame Meditation with Isis." I was guided to say some extra words for a lady at the workshop who needed to do some past life healing before she could benefit from what I was teaching with Athena. She came up to me after the meditation and said, "Did you know that I had been hung many times before in past lives and that I needed to clear the noose from around my neck?" I said, "Yes, I heard that message from the divine." I trusted and followed through. Kuan Yin has helped me expand the awareness of my purple crown chakra and trust the wisdom of the divine flowing into my chakras. I have learned that if you let go and trust, you will feel a sense of peace and complete self-fulfillment that is only earned through experience.

Kuan Yin also has helped me open my heart and learn to trust others as well as trust the divine source allowing me to have complete peace and self-fulfillment within all aspects of my life.

Having been schooled with a medical-scientific background, I asked for a lot of evidence that spirit existed and that what

I was feeling was real and amplified. I was taking my energy balancing course and there was an assignment in the course that had me weigh all of my healing crystals, one by one, on a food scale and then record the weight of the crystals before I used them on a client. Then after I had done an energy balancing session using the crystals on their chakras, I had to reweigh the crystals and record those results. I thought, *Okay, this will prove if the crystals really do work.* I weighed all nine of them with my food scale and recorded the weights.

I then placed them upon my client and proceeded to do a crystal healing session with them. As I took each crystal off the client's chakras, I would weigh them and record the weight beside the initial weight. I was amazed and dumbfounded at my results. The crystals did show different weights than I had recorded prior to the healing session. I weighed them a few times to make sure that I wasn't seeing things. Over and over I could see that the crystals that were placed on the chakras that were ready to release energies in fact weighed more than before the session. That meant that the crystals were storing the energies that were released by the chakras! I was now a firm believer in crystal healing and have never looked back since that experiment.

I also know that Kuan Yin has been with me helping me expand my heart chakra, allowing me to fully love and trust others in this lifetime. She has helped me open my heart chakra from my past wounds in this lifetime and past lives. She has been there sending love into my heart center, filling it up with her compassionate energy when I need it.

She wants me to spread the message that you can ask her to help you expand your heart and crown chakras, allowing your soul to trust the divine completely and to follow your bliss. She will help you release the self-critical shadow that is silently sabotaging your efforts and relationships.

Crystal Healing

Kuan Yin suggests that you may wish to place a pink rhodonite crystal in your left pocket to receive self-healing, love, and self-worth. You may also wish to place the rhodonite upon your heart chakra or solar plexus chakra (belly button) to promote a feeling of confidence using your talents and skills to help others along their path.

You may wish to use the blue kyanite crystal to strengthen and unify your physical being with a bridge to your spiritual being, allowing your trust and connection with the divine to be very strong and confident.

You can place the kyanite on your third-eye chakra, which is between your two physical eyes.

So with the combination of Kuan Yin's energy and the rhodonite and kyanite crystals, you will open up your heart center, expand your solar plexus (power center), and flourish into the beautiful, confident soul that you were intended to be here on Earth.

Affirmation

"May you have peace from divine connection and self-fulfillment."

Dedication

I would like to dedicate this chapter to my mother-in-law Barbara Mary Stafford Hughes who passed away in February 2008. Barbara was a very dear soul that showed compassion for all and loved everyone unconditionally.

Chapter 13

———— ❧ ————

Butterfly Maiden
Transformation

Color: Rainbow
Crystal: Herkimer Diamond

The Butterfly Maiden goddess is a Native American spirit goddess who will help you shed your cocoon, grow your beautiful wings, and fly to new heights! She oversees crops and gardens, ensuring that we have healthy food to consume for the year.

This goddess is often depicted as having long dark hair with dark skin. Beautiful colored wings of violet, indigo, yellow, orange, blue, and green, growing from the very center of the back of her heart chakra. She is very strong in nature and can help guide you through any transformations that you are ready and willing to go through.

Women have made many, many transformations, physically, mentally, spiritually, and energetically throughout the years on this Earth. We have the natural ability to go with the flow of change, if we are truly tuned in to out our feminine bodies. There are many cycles in life. We are like old oak trees going through cycles internally and shedding old ways externally. We have the ability to ground our roots deep into Mother Earth, gaining our stability and releasing our negative/lower energy into her earthly maternal soil. When we have our roots truly grounded, we can work

*our way up our chakras to the sacral chakra that
ignites passion within our creative centers, allowing
this energy to flow up to the solar plexus, which is our
power center. It is very important each and every day
as women that we stand in our power so we are stable
and flexible to maintain a healthy flow of energy in
our environments.*

One way to do this is to take some time first thing in the
morning while lying down or sitting in a cross-legged position.
See your solar plexus (belly button) area opening up wide to the
sunshine, breathe deeply, and on every inhalation see the yellow
sun rays filling up this center. See the diameter of this circle
getting wider and wider, filling up your midsection completely.
Physically feel the energy in this center growing and building.

Please keep seeing this yellow circle building and growing
and see it expanding to fill the room that you are in, then please
see it expanding to fill the town/city that you are residing in, and
then if you wish, see it expanding to fill the province or state that
this city or town is in. Then see these yellow rays expanding and
filling the world, sending yellow rays of sunshine to the universe
and infinity, connecting you to all sources of love and light.
You may even wish to do this daily love exercise outside in the
sunshine. Be careful not to look directly into the sun's rays.

After the activity, check to see how your body is physically
feeling. You may feel that you have an increase in energy to
tackle all of those daily tasks that you have been putting off, like
exercising, eating healthy, doing the laundry, getting groceries, or
making meals. Try this exercise each morning and then journal
your following days and see what a difference these five to ten
minutes can make to your daily activities. It will also affect your
encounters with all people during the day.

As women, sometimes we may be afraid to stand in our
power. This can stem from an association of cords from past
lifetimes of being very powerful and being executed for those
abilities. Know that it is safe now for you to be your true
powerful, loving self. May your intentions be of love and light
to all beings.

I have struggled with these roles of power in my life. Being an Aries, I will take on big projects, putting on events and then trying to do the registration, the marketing, the goody bags, organizing of musicians, booking the meeting room, etc. And in the end, when it comes down to my part in speaking at the event, I am tired. I have left this to the last minute trying to take care of all the other details. So my advice to you is to take time by yourself every day to do this solar plexus expansion and energy restructuring within your body and this will change the energy for the entire day. You will be able to focus a lot easier. You will also be able to accomplish a lot more tasks if you take a little time each morning to acknowledge that higher priestess energy with the help of sister sun.

Once you have done the expansion of the solar plexus exercise, you can ask the Butterfly Maiden to help assist you through any changes that you have wanted to make within your life. You may already know what it is that you want to change in your life; this could be your exercise habits, your occupation, your marriage, your eating habits, anything that you desire that will aid your life path in a positive way. You can also ask your higher self what your next step in transformation is.

Listen carefully for the guidance. You may get your answer by hearing the gentle guidance, or you may see a movie that will trigger something you feel you need to change. A friend may tell you something that resonates. It will all happen in divine time. True guidance is always loving and gentle, repeating over and over again until you hear it.

I was guided to start the process of transformation by quitting my job as a health information management analyst that I had held for fifteen years. I had my first daughter, Kayla, and tried to go back to work part-time during the evenings to keep the benefits, which included my pension and health insurance. Within a few weeks of this commitment I found myself calling home to my husband every few hours to see how my baby was doing. After a few weeks, I heard this voice say to me, "You only get to be with your baby once during their lifetime. They will grow up very fast." So I honored myself and decided to quit altogether and be a stay at home mother.

As you can imagine, this had a lot of consequences in my life. My personal income had now dropped to nothing and I had little or no time to myself. Being a wise one, I have that built-in need to spend some solitude time daily to refresh my energy and mind. I also realized how my self-worth took a toll in not being in a professional role. I did go through some depression not being around my hospital community that I had been my support system for the past fifteen years.

They had seen me fall in love, get engaged, get married, and then have my first baby. I did go to visit them regularly at first to keep those roots attached.

I did the right thing for my daughter and for myself! I will never regret quitting the part-time job to stay at home with her and see how quickly she changed and grew.

The one thing that I wished that I had known then was how all of this energy work could have benefited me so much along the path of my life.

I then had another daughter, Josie, three years later and decided that I wanted to start bringing in my own money and working outside the home part time. I went to a Mary Kay party at a friend's house and was immediately interested in knowing more details about how this mother of three was making her own money by doing Mary Kay cosmetic parties during the evenings when her husband was at home to watch the children. I thought, *Well this is the best of both worlds. I need to talk to this smart lady.*

Well this lady was Tannis Keeley from a nearby town in my area. She came over for coffee one afternoon and told me about this amazing business. I was interested and signed up immediately. I very quickly read over the entire business plan that Mary Kay Ash had set up and got to work.

My husband was very supportive of this new transformation that I was undergoing and watched the girls for me when I went out to do my classes. I immediately felt an increased sense of self-worth when I could see how applying makeup and taking some *me* time for many women was so empowering for them. They would leave the skin care class with smiles on their faces, as they had some quality girlfriend time and had nurtured their souls with love and beauty.

During the next twelve months, I accomplished my goal of becoming a senior sales director and won the triple excellence award, which is a very prestigious award presented annually.

I had women stopping and asking me how I became so successful so quickly. My response to them was that the previous year's Mary Kay seminar I had watched the women getting their awards on stage being treated like princesses and I wanted to have that. So sure enough, the very next year I did just that. I have always believed that you can do whatever you put your mind to. Don't listen to the naysayers. Surround yourself in your very own cocoon of support and love and you can make all of your dreams happen. This is how I did all of those things that the other consultants were wondering how I accomplished so much in so little time. I read the marketing plan and then set my daily business tasks to balance with my family life.

When I became pregnant with my third daughter, Erin, I once again was being guided to return to my true-life path and consider some changes.

I decided to resign as a sales director and spend time obtaining my natural health practitioner diploma, learning natural healing techniques and bringing forth my own ancient wisdom to share with other women in this lifetime.

I am truly grateful for what the Mary Kay business and women did for my life. I learned how to empower myself and how to create the energy in a team of women to help all women attain their goals in life and to support their changes. I am still very good friends with my sister goddess Tannis and know that we were divinely guided to meet on our paths and to grow separately but with each other's support, no matter where we are on our life path.

I know that the Butterfly Maiden was there by my side when I had to hand in my resignation at the hospital and hear all of the naysayers tell me that I was crazy for quitting a job that had a great pension plan and amazing benefits! She was there to support me and tell me that I wasn't crazy for making these changes.

I know that she was there for me when I decided to resign as a sales director and leave that dynamic group of women to once again delve into something completely new and out there, even though the naysayers were once again saying, "Why would you give up your customer base of three hundred women?" I just knew deep down that I had to honor my feminine wisdom and I had been getting this message for years to listen and to trust that everything would be okay.

Throughout each change in my life, sure I had wondered if I was making the right decision, especially when those around me weren't so supportive, but something deeper inside my soul would always reassure me that I was on the right path. Then things would easily fall into place affirming that I had made the right choice.

As women, we make many changes in our lives and at those times I am urging you to please ask the Butterfly Maiden for support. She will be there putting you into her cocoon of transformation, helping your heart heal from past life lessons and opening your heart center to move into the new adventures that await you.

Crystal Healing

You may wish to place the clear Herkimer quartz diamond upon your heart chakra when going through the process of transformation and ascension. This crystal will assist in the process of bringing high vibrational energy into your physical body allowing you to shed old thought patterns and release emotional baggage that may be stored within your heart chakra. This crystal will also support the amount of light energy that your body can utilize. Nurture your Herkimer like you would nurture a newborn, giving it lots of love and light.

Affirmation

"Please see her beautiful colorful wings as yours, helping you float through the winds of change with grace and dignity, and know that you will face these changes and that this goddess will assist you, if you wish, with love and grace!"

Dedication

I would like to dedicate this chapter to my youngest daughter, Erin Rachel Silver Hughes. You are a beautiful soul never afraid to soar to new unseen heights.

Chapter 14

———◦⊱✿⊰◦———

Kali

Honoring Cycles

Color: Eggplant
Crystal: Danburite

Kali is a powerful Hindu goddess who helps you release the old energy in your life and celebrate by bringing in new energy. She is very wise in dealing with preparing souls who are ready to leave their physical bodies and pass on to the spiritual realm. She also helps assist in pregnancy and bringing new life onto Mother Earth. Kali assists in the rebirth of spirit and reincarnation. She has a very deep relationship with Mother Earth. She is the goddess to call upon when you want support to reach the next goal in your life that feels unattainable to you.

Sisters and brothers, call upon me when you are needing to move forward on your path and you don't feel strong enough to put one foot in front of the other. I will be there gently pushing you through your limited belief systems that you may have about your self-worth and capabilities. I can see your full potential and that you are fully qualified to fill those big shoes that you have dreamt about your entire life. Allow your imagination to soar and let go of all limiting beliefs about yourself! Close your eyes for a moment, take a deep breath, bring in the divine energy fill up all of the cells in your body, and connect the soles of your feet with Mother Earth and the top of your head with Father Sky. Allow the white divine energy to flow up and down your vertebral column. Feel your body become very light and see your spirit leaving your body. Feel your arms above your head flying high above Mother Earth. Please know that you are safe during this journey. Now ask your spirit guides, God, Kali, and Mother Earth to show you your life as it would be when you have accomplished your ultimate goal! Take a few minutes soaring above all Earth bound life. Look at all aspects of yourself from this higher point of view. How do you feel? Tap into your heart for a minute and note how you are feeling. Notice how large your aura may be during this process of future dream envisioning. You are this beautiful divine soul that is shining light upon Mother Earth. You can accomplish anything that you wish. You have the divine connections and support!

Now please put forth the intention to come back into your physical body and back to this moment in time. You may feel refreshed and enlightened.

You may wish to write out your goals and give yourself some time lines to accomplish these tasks. Then you may wish to sign your name at the bottom of the paper and put it in a beautifully decorated box with a clear quartz crystal or a rose quartz crystal. This can be your dream box. You may do this exercise each time you feel that you need my support to move forward on your path.

Kali is the goddess who has assisted me when I lost many family members during a very short period of time a few years ago. My aunt Sharon was a very special lady in my life. She was diagnosed with cancer in her uterus many years ago. I had lost touch with her over my younger years but then reconnected with her at a funeral of a man who had lived in our community. She told me about her cancer and what treatments she was doing at that time. I told her about the healing work that I was doing and asked if she would mind being a client for the practicum that I needed to finish to obtain my certificates. She agreed and we began truly getting to know each other again.

We would spend hours talking while I was practicing my reflexology on her. I would intuitively place certain crystals on her chakras during her healing session. She was very good at communicating with me about what she was feeling around the energy and very helpful in my natural healing learning process.

During these months I was taking reflexology, aromatherapy, crystal healing, hot stone massage, energy balancing, European Lymphatic Massage, Angel Therapy Practitioner®, and Angel Therapy Medium®. My aunt Sharon was willing to be a loving participant in all of my learning. She told me that she was having trouble sleeping at night and loved rose oil so I eagerly found a synergistic recipe, which could aid in her rest at night. As I was researching the benefits and contraindications for the rose absolute oil, I saw a phrase that caught my eye: "Will help the spirit go toward the light at the time of death."

Intuitively, I knew I was reconnected with my aunt at this time, at the new reawakening of our relationship. I also knew that she had in fact already chosen to leave her physical body and that I could help facilitate her journey along with way and that she would be an amazing teacher for me along the way!

My aunt and uncle never had any children of their own. They were both loving souls full of laughter and wit. My aunt had tried many alternative therapies, Chinese acupuncture and herbs, alternative chemotherapy, reiki, and much more.

During her last few months, I committed to going over to her home every other day to do some hands-on healing to help relieve her from the pain that she was feeling. Her cancer had metastasized and spread to a large portion of her abdomen. She had a very large blood clot in her thigh and had limited mobility. My friend Christy, who is a Chinese doctor, would also attend these sessions with my aunt Sharon and me. She would do acupuncture for pain relief while I was running energy through the needles and my aunt's body wherever I felt guided to put my hands during the session. I also used crystals and essential oils during our sessions. Even though I knew that my aunt knew that she only had limited time left here on Earth, she would always make Christy and me laugh, and tell us some wisdom that she had thought of during her day lying in bed.

One day we could hear an owl on the roof of her house hooting his beautiful music. My aunt said that there was an owl's nest near their home with some baby owls in it and that they loved to watch them. I received a message from the owls that this was going to be a symbol for us to communicate with each other after she had passed. I told my aunt the message and she agreed!

Every day that I would leave my aunt's house, she would thank me from the bottom of her heart. I knew that she looked forward to this time with me and I too cherished being with her. I was amazed at how loving and kind she was even though I knew she was in so much pain every day! She handled the whole process of dying with grace and love.

Soon it came time for her to go into the hospital for palliative care as she needed the extra help from the nurses and she needed morphine to help her with the increased pain as the cancer was spreading throughout her entire body. My uncle was an amazing supportive husband to my aunt throughout the entire process! They had a special kind of love that you don't see very often.

Each day I would visit her in the local hospital. She was making the nurses laugh with her stories and bright spirit. As the days progressed, I could see that my aunt's body was wasting away, so I decided to call my mom to come and say good-bye to Aunt Sharon. My mom was in Arizona, USA, which was a minimum three-hour airplane trip away.

Every time that I would leave her, I would say good-bye as if it might be the last time I would see her. I felt so grateful to be able to tell her what she had meant to me. I felt a sense of peace and completeness when I would leave her, knowing that I had no regrets. I was so fortunate to be able to learn so much from her lessons on dying, as from my own learning about healing, life, and death.

During this time my mother-in-law, Barbara, was diagnosed with colon cancer. One day Barb was babysitting our girls while Stephen and I went out for a movie and dinner. When we arrived home, I asked her how she was doing and she told me that her foot was really hurting. She knew that I was taking my natural health practitioner diploma. I asked her to show me exactly where on her foot the pain was, as I might be able to relate it to a body part with my reflexology training. It was the reflex point that corresponded to the colon. So I then asked her a few more questions about her bowel function. She told me that her bowel movements weren't regular and that she had a lot of diarrhea lately. I explained that I thought she should go to the doctor as soon as possible as this wasn't normal. My knowing that there was something very wrong was very strong.

Barb never liked to be a bother to anyone. When she phoned to get an appointment with her family physician, the receptionist told her that there was no opening with her doctor but she could wait a few weeks and see the doctor when she was scheduled to have her annual physical. Not wanting to be persistent, Barb said that she would wait. My gut was telling me that she needed to get in sooner than that, but I didn't know how assertive to be with the situation. She eventually ended up throwing up constantly and couldn't pass any food through her colon. She had an emergency CT scan of her abdomen and the results came back that she had a complete blockage of her colon and that it had metastasized to her mesentery around her colon. There was also a tiny spot on her lungs, which was suspicious for cancer.

A few weeks later, Barb had a large portion of her colon removed along with the blockage. She told me this story when I went to visit her. While she was waiting to go into surgery, she had this amazing nurse who was prepping her. Barb asked this nurse how long she had worked at this hospital and she told her it was a very long time. Barb knew that my birth grandfather was the CEO of that hospital many years ago, so she asked this nurse if she knew of him. The nurse replied that she did know my birth grandfather and they were in fact good friends, until he moved away. Barb then told the nurse that the CEO's granddaughter was her daughter-in-law. The nurse teared up and said, "I remember when that little baby was born. He had arranged her adoption. I wondered what had ever happened to that little baby girl and now I know." Barb teared up also and said, "I will have you know that my daughter-in-law, Velva Dawn, has three amazing little girls and is doing fine!" When Barb told me this story, I had goose bumps everywhere as I knew it was no coincidence that Barb thought to ask this nurse about my birth grandfather. This was a sign from the angels and Kali that we are always surrounded by divine love and support.

My mother-in-law never did leave the hospital for long after that surgery. She had many postoperative complications. She had blood clots in both of her lungs postoperatively. Barb and I were very close. We had lived in the same yard and had talked daily on the telephone or in person until her hospitalization. I knew that she was another amazing teacher who had entered my life.

I soon knew that I was entering a cycle of my life where I was learning at a very fast pace about life, death, and rebirth. I felt as though I needed to learn about these cycles, as I had not lost a lot of family members or friends to death by this time in my life.

I found it very difficult to see Barb in the hospital, as she loved to be outdoors with the plants and flowers and tending to her garden. She was a very social woman, kind and gentle, and listened with a nonjudgmental ear whenever anyone needed to be heard. During her stay in the hospital, there was some miscommunication with the medical team and her true diagnosis was never told to her or the family until later. She went to see an oncologist one more time in the city and he told her straight that she couldn't do chemotherapy as her physical body was too weak to go through the drugs.

My aunt Sharon was getting weaker and weaker by the day, letting go of her physical body and strengthening her spirit. I saw her daily and could see it was soon time for her to pass over. I had told her how grateful I was for all of the lessons I had learned from her and loved her infinitely. She passed while I was away from the hospital, but I rushed there as soon as my mom phoned to tell me the news. I knew that my mom helped Aunt Sharon pass over. She is an angel who helps others go to the light during this difficult time. When I arrived, I looked around the hospital room to see if I could see her spirit. I could hear her saying, "It will be okay. Please comfort your uncle and everyone."

She told me that she knew we would always be able to communicate as I had the ability to speak to spirits as a medium. She also told me that the owl was our sign that she was near me and to keep an eye out for her. She said, "Good-bye, kiddo. I love you and will miss you! I am no longer in pain and am in complete peace and thank you for all of your spiritual healings that have led me to this place of surrender and infinite love."

Aunt Sharon's funeral was on a Monday afternoon in January 2008. I felt drained and sad but was at peace knowing that I could still talk with her whenever I wanted to. That evening we received a phone call from Barb's family physician. He told us that there was a miscommunication and that Barb only had a little time left. Her lungs were filling up with fluid and her cancer was spreading rapidly. He suggested that we gather all of the family, take photos, and say our good-byes, as she was terminally ill and wouldn't be with us for long.

Some family members were in shock with this news, but I had received this message when her foot was hurting months ago. Barb knew that she could be of more help in spirit form and that it was her time to go.

I was angry after that phone call from Barb's doctor, even though I knew it was coming. I didn't know how our family could deal with all of this grief at one time. Barb was given a weekend pass to come home to see all of her family and friends. I went shopping to get food for everyone who would be coming to see Barb. As I was driving up the gravel road to our house to unload my groceries, I saw my father-in-law wheeling Barb in her wheelchair into the house. Her head was down and I could see that she had given up all hope.

My gut was screaming at me to go down and see Barb now, but, feeling the grief so fresh from my aunt Sharon passing, I couldn't go at that moment. I had stopped by to visit Barb on Monday after Aunt Sharon's funeral while she was still in the hospital, and I knew that Stephen and I would be going to see Barb the next day, which was Saturday morning, and we would take our three girls to say good-bye to her.

That night, the night that I ignored my gut feeling, at 2:18 a.m. the phone rang and I knew Barb had left her physical body. My husband said that Barb had collapsed, wasn't breathing, and that they had called an ambulance. I sat straight up in bed. My heart was pounding and I immediately called out to Barb's spirit while I waited to hear what happened. My gut told me that she had exited.

Stephen came back to the house and said that the ambulance had arrived and that his mom was gone. We were angry and in shock and disbelief. Stephen's dad asked us to make the phone calls to let family and friends know that she had passed.

Everyone was angry and in shock when we made those phone calls. The hardest part for me was telling our three daughters that their loving grandma had passed away and that she would no longer be in their lives in physical form; Kayla was eleven years old, Josie was eight years old, and Erin was five years old. My girls were very close to Grandma Barb as we ranched together and lived very close to one another.

Then one day while I was sitting quietly I could feel that Barb was trying to talk to me. So I sat quietly and then I saw her with a gentle smile on her face. I said, "Why did you go and do that?" I was angry about how she exited without closure for anyone. She said, "I am sorry dear but that was the only way I could leave. It was too hard to say good-bye to everyone so I chose not to! I need you to give some messages to family members for me, as I know you can." I sat and journaled the messages in my journal for her.

After some time had passed, I did pass these messages on even though I knew that some might judge me for being able to communicate with the deceased. My intuition and medical background told me that Barb had released a blood clot and died from a stroke, so I asked her if this was true and she said, "Yes, I had to go immediately as I didn't want to suffer anymore, nor did I wish anyone else around me to suffer, so I chose this quick exit point."

Finally, the grief had taken its toll on my physical and spiritual body. I had gained forty pounds in a few months as I was eating to hide the painful feelings I was having. I heard Kali say to me, "Dear one, this is a very emotional and hard cycle of time for you to endure, but you are strong enough to handle it, and that is why it is happening this way! There are some more deaths to come soon, so please use your intuitive wisdom to assist where you are needed. You are a very strong woman and you can handle this!"

Crystal Healing

You may wish to place the white danburite crystal above your crown chakra to activate your frequencies to connect with the angels and higher realms. Danburite will allow your spirit to tap into the veil that separates us from the divine and it will open up the unseen world of loving spirits that surround us.

Affirmation

"Remember when one soul passes over we have an amplified source with the divine."

Dedication

I would like to dedicate this chapter to my aunt, Sharon Palosky, who passed away in January 2008. She taught me how to have grace through all things in life.

Chapter 15

Mawu

Divine Mother Earth

Color: Brown
Crystal: Seraphinite

Mawu is a West African Earth goddess who has great knowledge on how to supply our needs without harming our great Mother Earth. She has a very strong connection to Mother Earth and can tap into her vibration to help transmute and amplify her needs to all souls that are willing to help lessen the negative impact on her planet.

I can assist you in finding environmentally safe cleaning products. I can give you recipes using natural organic sources to clean your home. They are safe for your physical body as well as Mother Earth's body, the planet. I will remind you to take your reusable grocery shopping bags with you when you go shopping so that we can lighten the load on the landfills. I can help guide you to use crystals to grid your land and home to heal the soil from chemicals and pollutants. I will guide you to natural ways of growing your own garden full of fruits, vegetables, and herbs to make healthy, high-vibrating meals for yourself and your loved ones. I have many recipes of wisdom to help heal, decrease pollution, and use alternative choices so we can all live our lives on Earth.

Mawu has guided me to grid our family ranch with crystals to help heal the land by increasing the vibration of the earthly elements. That coincides with increasing a healthy auric field for Mother Earth.

Years ago, before they knew better, my husband's family used chemicals to spray the weeds that they considered encroachments on the land. I grew up as a farmer's daughter where my father used chemicals to grow and fertilize his crops, as do many other farmers around the world. I was diagnosed with asthma at the age of thirty-seven. I am certain that this is a symptom of the chemicals, second-hand cigarette smoke, and living near a flaming gas well for many years.

My first message from Mawu was to speak up and strongly insist that my husband and father-in-law please not use chemicals to get rid of the weeds on the land. As you can imagine, this request caused a stir, as this would be changing what they had done for years. I was grateful as they did shift fairly quickly and started to mow the weeds with a bush mower and quit using chemicals.

Mawu guided me to go out and purchase eight clear quartz crystals and eight rose quartz crystals and a clear quartz pyramid crystal. I bought these and then cleansed the clear quartz for a minimum of seven days in water with a pinch of Dead Sea salt (clear quartz is one crystal that needs to be cleansed for seven days as it could be programmed by someone else). I cleansed the rose quartz in the water also.

I was then guided to hold the crystals up to my third eye and ask the matrix of the crystals if they would be willing to hold the vibration of Mawu's healing to help increase the vibration of Mother Earth's aura. I received affirmation that the crystals were willing to do this healing. I was then guided to place a clear quartz crystal along with one rose quartz crystal outside in the soil at each of the four corners of our house. Before burying each of the crystals, I would hold them up to the sky and ask Mawu for her blessing and then place the crystals in a shallow hole that I had dug to begin their activation of the healing grid that Mawu guided me to do for our house, the ranch, and the planet.

I started at one corner of the house and then rotated in a clockwise direction, blessing and gently burying these healing crystals. I then used a clear quartz pyramid crystal inside my house in the very center of my home in one of my ornamental Buddha's hands. I could see white beams of light coming from all four corners of our house, transmuting into the clear quartz pyramid. This clear quartz pyramid is then connected to a larger divine blueprint and will be amplified for healing around the universe.

Within hours of placing this crystal grid around our house, I could see the energy shifting within each of my family members. My husband's energy was very resistant to this high vibration and I could see that he was having trouble making decisions and resting. I intuitively knew that eventually his energy would embrace the higher vibration once he was tired of resisting. I gave him a pyrite crystal to carry in his pocket to help him ground.

I also noticed that all three of my daughters were shifting each in their own way with this grid, so I gridded different crystals under their beds as I was guided to do so from Mawu and their spirit guides. I had also programmed this clear quartz pyramid to gather all negative and lower energies that might come into our home and release them up into Father Sky to recycle this energy into love and light.

I love watching different people enter our home for a visit and seeing them shift while they are here. I often hear comments from friends who have visited our home after the gridding—they have made significant changes for the better in their lives.

Mawu then guided me to take four clear quartz crystals and four rose quartz crystals and bury one of each of them at each of the four corners of our five-thousand-acre ranch. My husband Stephen came with me, as did our three dogs, for this afternoon journey. We headed toward the northwest corner or the ranch on our low-impact ATV with crystals in tow. As we approached this corner, I saw the feathers of a deceased red-tail hawk in the corner, and I believe that this was an affirmation that we were doing the right thing by healing this land. I knew that this journey was going to take quite a few hours as it takes time to cross five thousand acres, over streams and grasslands along the way. Stephen opened a shallow hole in the corner and I held the crystals up for programming from Mawu and the divine. I gently placed the crystals in the soil and laid the blanket of grass down for renewal.

We then traveled south to the very southwest corner of the parcel of land. At this corner, a white-tailed deer went running by us. This was my second affirmation during the gridding. Then we headed east toward the southeast corner of the ranch. There was a family of owls living in a group of trees near this corner, being my third affirmation. I gridded that corner and then headed to the final northeast corner of the land where I placed the last of the crystals under the divine soil. I looked up into the sky and saw the most beautiful colors radiating from the sunshine onto the white clouds. I knew that we had now increased the vibration of our land and house and that we were now tapped into a divine energetic blueprint of universal energy that would be connected to all of the great ancient wonders of the world to help amplify the spiritual healing of the universe and to aid in the ascension of all souls!

I was amazed at how I could immediately feel how the energy had shifted on our piece of Mother Earth and was truly grateful for the guidance from Mawu to help do my part in healing and ascension on Earth.

I have had clients and friends tell me that they can feel the divine energy from our land miles away when they are driving toward our ranch. I very much can sense this also when I am out shopping for the day where there is a large population of people. I can feel all of the weight lifting off my auric field as I drive toward our house.

So please ask Mawu for help if you are guided to grid your house and/or property with crystals to tap into this divine blueprint connection to help heal the world and assist with the ascension.

Crystal Healing

You may wish to place the seraphinite crystal upon your heart chakra to send healing energy out to the universe to help heal

Mother Earth. Seraphinite will help bring forth any underlying causes of imbalance within yourself and the Earth before they are able to manifest into disease. This crystal will connect us to the highest realms of Spirit bringing this high vibration into our physical body which will then allow us to ground this healing into actions to alleviate stress on Mother Earth. Please accept the healing that seraphinite offers and be a part in Mawu's healing of the universe.

Affirmation

"We are all one body living on the co-creative energy of Mother Earth. All of our decisions and actions will affect her auric field, so please choose wisely for all of us. We are one."

Dedication

I would like to dedicate this chapter to my daughter Josie Eira Silver Hughes, who loves to be on the land connecting with her animals and crystals.

Photo of the sky after I was done gridding
the ranch with crystals.

Chapter 16

Athena

The Warrior Within

Color: Fuchsia
Crystal: Hematite

Athena is the Greek goddess whose strong qualities are to ignite the warrior within. She is the daughter of the mighty Zeus. Her power animals are a white owl and a black pigeon. She is one of the protector goddesses. She is very wise and will teach you how to empower yourself using your own intuition and to trust yourself.

> *Sisters, you know what the right answer is. Tap into your soul asking your question and then listen for the answer. Be patient; you soul is a very wise intelligent center knowing all things. Step inside and get to know this part of yourself. Take time each day to go within and seek your answers. We empower ourselves when we get the answer from within. Trust is a very important key in strengthening your intuitive awareness. You were born with all of the tools that you need to follow your life path with accuracy and joy. Ask me to help you sharpen these tools. I am here with you just waiting.*

I first started to really become aware of my intuition about eleven years ago. I was having coffee with a friend and she looked deep into my eyes and asked me if I thought that there was life after death. I thought about it for a minute and then said, "Yes, I believe that does exist." She asked me if I believed in past lives. I said, "I'm not sure but would like to know more about that topic."

This friend was doing her crystal healing course and asked me if I would like a crystal healing session with her. I gladly took her up on her offer and was amazed at what I felt during the ninety-minute treatment. She had placed many crystals on all seven of my chakras and I had a couple in the palm of my hands. I remember specifically that she had placed a tiger's eye crystal on each of my thighs. I felt very light during the crystal session and could vaguely feel the energy flowing down my body out of my feet. I remember when she went to remove the tiger's eye crystals they were stuck on my thighs. She said to me, "You store a lot of stuff in your legs. It's important that you do some sort of physical exercise to keep your energy flowing." I found this very interesting and wanted to learn more about crystal healing.

Within a couple of days, I bought a book on crystals and read the entire book from front to back in an evening. Reading this book was like a remembering for me. I could easily remember the colors of the crystals, their names, and their healing properties, yet I had only read the book once! I was a bit baffled by this happening and was starting to think that having a past life could be possible. I continued working with crystals, trying different ones on my body and feeling how the energy would flow in different patterns depending on how I placed the crystals. I now knew that I had used crystals to heal others and myself in many past lives.

I continued to receive crystal healings from my friend Marie for a few months. I started to notice that she was becoming controlling of my time and friendship with others. On one visit to her house, I was sitting in the living room and the kitchen light switch would flicker on and off, and there was no one standing there. I was a bit freaked out by this and asked her what was happening. She said that she liked to pick up deceased spirits from graveyards and help them go to the light! You can imagine how I felt. I was feeling very unsure of this energy. I knew that this was not something that I wanted to experience in my lifetime.

A few months later my family and I went up again to visit Marie and her family. My husband and I were sleeping upstairs in one room, and Marie's daughter and my three girls were sleeping in the other bedroom upstairs. About 4:00 a.m. I heard feet running across the hardwood floor in the children's playroom upstairs. I bolted straight up in bed, eyes wide open, and asked my husband if he heard a noise. He said, "Yes one of the children must be up and playing." I had a bad feeling in my stomach and thought if he heard the noise, and it wasn't just me who heard it, then he might be right. My clairaudience was very clear at this point and he was not open to using his clair's in any way, shape, or form, as of yet. So I slowly got out of bed and walked across the hallway to open the door to the where the girls were all sleeping. I opened their door and, to my surprise, they were all sound asleep!

I felt very uneasy and thought, *Okay, she has another spirit who is playing in the toy room.* I went to the door of the toy room. It was very quiet and the room was pitch black. I knew my intuition was right and that there was a little boy's spirit in that room playing. I went back to bed and told my husband what I thought and he was also very uneasy about the situation.

The next morning, I asked Marie if she had heard the little boy running in the playroom last night. She said, "No, I told him not to bother anyone. I will have to talk to him." At this point, I was ready to pack up everyone and head straight for home! I knew one thing for sure: that this energy was not resonating with me at all. I didn't like it!

When we were leaving Marie's home, she said to me, "We need to stop by the bookstore in town before you head home, as there is a book that I want to give you before you go home." We stopped by the local mall and she went in and bought me Doreen Virtue's book *Angel Medicine*. She handed it to me and said, "Here, read this and see what you remember." I started reading it on our ten-hour drive home, expecting to have this huge light-bulb moment of what my past lives might be!

I was really trying to decide if Marie was leading me down the wrong road with all of this energy healing that she was doing. I knew one thing for sure and that was that I didn't like earthbound spirits around me. I had previously arranged for my friend Marie to come to my home for a week to do some crystal healings on some of my clients. I knew how much I enjoyed my crystal healings and wanted to share that healing with others. I also wanted to help Marie get her business going.

I had booked five to six clients a day for a week for Marie to see in my treatment room in our house. I picked her up at the nearby airport and drove her to our family ranch.

I noticed that when she greeted my husband that she winked at him, hugged him, and then said, "Hi, sexy!" I thought, *Okay, has this flirting been happening for the past few years and I just didn't want to see it because she was supposed to be my best friend?* My gut was telling me that yes, this was very inappropriate and to be watchful of what she was up to.

I had booked my husband in for a crystal healing with Marie on the Thursday of that week. Her sessions were slotted to take a maximum of ninety minutes. I had a bad feeling in my stomach before he went down for his treatment that something was not right. I came down with him to the treatment room where Marie was conducting her healing sessions, as I wanted to sit in on this session so that I could learn more about crystal healing. I knew that confidentiality wouldn't be an issue as he was my husband.

Well, to my surprise, Stephen asked me to leave. He said he would rather that I wasn't there for his session. I was very hurt by this but went upstairs to wait. I had given Stephen a necklace that had the OM symbol on it a few months before that, and he was wearing it during his session with Marie. As I was upstairs waiting, my stomach was in knots and I felt like someone had punched me in the gut! I could also feel this warm sensation in my stomach that I had never remembered experiencing before. I kept hearing that something wasn't right in that healing session. This was my very first strong gut feeling that something was very wrong!

Stephen's crystal healing session took two and half hours with Marie. This was a red flag for me, as to why was his session longer than anyone else's. When he came up the stairs he wouldn't look me in the eyes. He avoided eye contact and told me that he had to go outside. Second red flag! When Marie came upstairs, she was giving me the cold shoulder. I asked her how Stephen's healing session went and she said, "I can't share that information with you. It is confidential." I said, "You have to be kidding me, Marie. Why are you pulling the confidentiality card on me now when we have shared many other things, or so I thought, in our friendship?" Third red flag!

Now I knew something had gone very wrong during that healing session. When Stephen came inside after a few hours, I immediately walked up to him and took off his OM necklace and flushed it down the toilet. I wasn't sure why I was doing this but knew deep inside my soul that Marie had done some negative programming to his necklace during his healing session with her. I also began flushing many crystals that she had given me, as I was now wondering if she had programmed these crystals with negative energy.

That night Stephen and I talked for a long time and he admitted that Marie was directing him down the road that she would be a better wife for him than I was. During the healing session, she was saying negative things about me to him.

Fourth and final red flag for me! Okay I got it: she wanted my life and my husband! I could feel the goddess flame burning within my solar plexus ready for combat. I knew that Athena was by my side ready to help me confront this situation with my so-called best friend!

I knew that our friendship was over and I needed to stand up for my family and myself.

Stephen talked to Marie that morning and told her that he loved me and that he didn't know why she was trying to manipulate our marriage. She acted in denial as to why Stephen would be telling her that he loved his wife! He could see what she was trying to do and was furious with her and himself for being so naive!

I also confronted Marie that morning, telling her that she overstepped her boundaries with me in many ways! She glared at me with her piercing eyes and said, "How did I do that?" I said, "You know exactly what you were trying to do! I finally figured out your plan!" I told her that I had flushed Stephen's OM pendant down the toilet and she put her hands over her face. As she was sitting down, she kept saying, "Oh no, this will change my plan, this will change everything. You wrecked it!" This was my affirmation that I had done the right thing. I believe to this day that she had programmed his OM pendant with a spell of negative energy to end our marriage, so that she could have him!

We didn't speak very much at all for the one day that Marie had left at my home until her healing sessions were complete. I could feel that I was surrounded by God's love, many warrior goddesses, archangels, and angels all protecting me and my family from her negative intentions and energy.

As I drove her to the airport, I knew that this would be one of the last planned times that we would see each other in this lifetime. Marie cried as I walked away and got into my car to drive home. She left me a few threatening phone calls in the weeks following this incident.

Within a day of Marie leaving, I had complete clarity of what she was doing to me with her ill intentions. I could see that she was cutting me off from my friends, one that I had been a friend with for forty years. She tried to tell me that this girlfriend was jealous of me and that I should no longer communicate with her if I wanted to grow spiritually. She was isolating me from those around me who loved me and knew right from wrong. She wanted my husband and would stop at nothing to get what she wanted.

I know that we ask for certain lessons in our life for our own learning. I learned a few things from this encounter with Marie.

One was seeing the difference between living in the light versus hiding in the dark. Another one was manifesting your wishes through love and light with God and all beings of love and light or using black magic to get what you want. I also learned how strong my intuition is and that I am always protected by beings of love and light and strong warrior goddesses when I need them. I also learned that there are certain energies that I choose to not engage or learn about.

An affirmation that I received a few weeks after Marie had left was from Dion Fortune's book *How to Protect Yourself from a Psychic Attack*. I picked it up and went right to the page that explained how to get rid of an amulet that had been programmed with a negative vibration was to drop it into deep water or flush it down the toilet if you aren't near deep water. This was just another divine message for me that we always know what to do in any situation. Just trust!

I am grateful to Marie taking part in this life lesson for me and for propelling me on my intuitive healing path. I have grown in leaps and bounds from this relationship but no longer wish to learn any more lessons of this sort!

Crystal Healing

You may wish to place the silver hematite, polished or raw, at your feet or on your root chakra that is at the base of your spine. The hematite can be used to pull stray energy down through the meridians to the root chakra and then recycle these energies to Mother Earth. Hematite is one of the most effective stones for grounding your physical body. You may also wish to see a silver hematite shield in front of your physical body and behind it to protect your energy field from any unwanted energies. You may also wish to visualize some rose quartz crystals on your protective shield to radiate love to all those with whom you might come into contact during the day. Hematite is very beneficial in grounding you so that the light can enter your body.

Affirmation

"Never be afraid of anything or anyone. Know that you are always more powerful and that the vibration of love will also aid in protecting whenever needed. Remember to invite the warrior within you to come forth to assist you."

Dedication

I would like to dedicate this chapter to my crystal healing friend Debi McKee.

Chapter 17

———⸕⸕———

Aphrodite
Feminine Energy

Color: Orange
Crystal: Raw Blue Aquamarine

Aphrodite is the Greek goddess of passion and sexuality. She will help awaken the masculine energy within your body to work with the feminine and ignite the passion within your sacral chakra. She is often associated with the planet Venus. Aphrodite will balance the yin and yang within each of us, male or female. She also helps women become more aware and comfortable with their own physical bodies and sexual essence.

We need to celebrate our feminine curves and dance our energy into high vibrating patterns to help bring harmony to the masculine and feminine energy within our souls. We need to awaken the true classic feminine matriarchal essence that has been sleeping for centuries due to the power of the patriarchal patterns. The female energy is hungry and is craving passion and creativity. Mother Earth is asking each of us to take a part in this mission to help her unfold and spread this passion throughout the universe as a collaboration that will aid all of us on our life paths. This way we can all live with true passion using our talents and intuition in the purest forms. We all need to connect to the fiery sexual energy in our sacral chakras. We

can do this by using dance of any type. Movement
to increase the flow of energy into this orange center
and will bring forth a sense of excitement and power
within oneself.

It is time to heal our sacral chakras from any wounds that
we have encountered in this lifetime or past lifetimes. We need
to celebrate our feminine and balance it with the grounded
masculine.

Many people have a history of some sort of sexual abuse in
their lifetime. My story of sexual abuse started approximately at
the age of nine years old. My parents had a good friend's son
babysit my brother and me. I will give him the name of Carl
for confidentiality purposes. He said he had a fun game to play
with my brother and me. He said we had to play the game in
my bedroom on the bed. My brother was two years younger
than I was. As soon as we went into my bedroom, my stomach
started turning and I felt very scared. He told both of us that we
had to take off all of our clothes and that if we didn't do as he
said that he would tell my parents that we had done something
bad. We would get into trouble from them too!

I did this reluctantly while he touched my private parts with
his private parts. There was no penetration during this event,
which I am thankful for. After a few minutes, I said I didn't want
to play this game anymore and I got dressed and locked myself
in the bathroom for a long time.

I remember telling my mom soon after that event that I
didn't want Carl to babysit us anymore because he was mean.
She asked me why, but I could hear his words in my head: "If
you tell your mom you will get in a lot of trouble next time I
babysit you." I never told her what Carl did to us, until thirty
years later.

This was a hard situation as our families were friends. We
camped together, played cards, and visited at each other's houses
frequently. After that event, when we would visit Carl's family
I would always sit at the table with my parents, especially if he
was around. He must have felt my power, as he never touched

me again after that day. But the damage was already done. What he had done to me that day changed the course of my actions with men throughout the rest of my life.

When I was fifteen years old I started at a new high school in a different town. I was nervous to meet all of these new people and to take a different bus. I was from a very small hamlet of sixty people and grew up on a mixed farm of cattle and grain. I was very naive compared to other girls my age.

There was a boy in grade twelve who had asked me on my first official date. I will give him the name of Josh to conceal his identity. My girlfriend and I got ready at my house, excited and giggling, listening to music and doing our hair. We decided that we should take a bottle of vodka from my parents' liquor cabinet to help settle our nerves as this seemed to be what kids did in high school. The drive to the party was only fifteen minutes from our home, as it was being held at my parents' friends' house in a small hamlet. Josh and his friend picked up my girlfriend and me in his little sports car. We were off on our double date for the first time.

My girlfriend and I quickly drank the vodka straight to calm the butterflies in our stomachs. The next thing that I can remember is getting out of the car at the party, barely able to walk, slurring my words, and seeing double visions of everything. I remember my mom's friend asking me if I was okay and I said, "Yes." I quickly went outside to avoid her, as I didn't want her to see me so drunk. There was a lot of drama happening at this high school party, lots of crying from other friends, and lots of drinking. Then I was in the backseat of Josh's car being raped. I remember yelling, "Stop!" when I came to and then I would lose consciousness. I also remember seeing other boys looking at us through the back windows of the car and thinking that this was terrible, and that I somehow had to gain control of myself to stop this!

The next morning I awoke and had hoped that last night was a bad nightmare. As soon as I moved my body and sensed how sore I was, I knew that it wasn't a bad dream. The horrific events had actually happened. The next week at school everyone was pointing at me as I walked down the hallways and was talking about what happened that night. A few people in the community had somehow turned a date rape, where I was the victim, into me being called a slut. I felt so much shame and regret for that night.

I now realize that the scars of being sexually assaulted by Carl at the age of nine were weighing on my physical body and energy body in many ways. I never admitted to myself that I was in fact date-raped until I was about nineteen years old. Before that I had convinced myself, as did the community, that I had asked for it because I was drinking! I had been carrying this shame from when I was a little girl until just a few years ago.

A few years ago I finally told my parents what Carl had done to me when he was babysitting. I knew that this would be hard for them to hear after all of these years, and the fact that this boy was one of their best friend's sons. When I did tell them, they were very hurt and weren't sure how to deal with it all. This truth then led me to confess to them that Josh had date-raped me and that we should have laid charges against him at that time. I had kept all of these secrets inside of me because I felt so much shame and I thought that they would think less of me if I told them.

My parents took some time to take in all of this information and absorb what I had told them. Our relationship did go through some very rocky patches during this time, but I felt so free and light letting go of these secrets. My relationship with my parents is now based on trust, love, and gratitude, and for this I am truly grateful. Sometimes we must speak our truths and let go of the reactions that we might face when we allow our true self to emerge.

I have been working with Aphrodite to develop my trust in intimate relationships and encounters with men period. After those events, I felt as though I had lost my power and only attracted men who would treat me with no respect. I was always wondering why I was attracting men who didn't respect me! When I met my husband, he was a very gentle man and did treat me with respect at the beginning of our relationship. We had one very difficult night when we were both drinking at the local bar. We were engaged at that time, and he accused me of flirting with one of my ex-boyfriends while we were out that night. The argument escalated into him choking me and yelling all types of profanities at me. I called my parents to tell them what had happened and that I needed to call off the wedding. My mom suggested that I call my cousin and ask her to come and get me as she lived only thirty minutes away.

That is what I did and Donna drove out to get me from Stephen's house that night. I packed up some of my stuff and we left. I made it home and got into bed when I heard the doorbell ring. I knew it was Stephen! He was saying he was sorry over and over again. I finally let him in the door and told him it was late, and that he shouldn't have been driving. I made the decision that he could sleep on the floor downstairs and we would talk again in the morning when we both had sober thoughts.

I decided that it would be best to talk with the minister of our church about what had happened. Some of my friends and family had chalked up the event to alcohol and told me not to worry about it. We were both intoxicated!

My minister really encouraged Stephen to get some anger management counseling, which he did, one time. She strongly urged me to call off the wedding for now. I told her that I couldn't call off the wedding as it was all planned and that everyone would be disappointed in me if I did this.

She strongly counseled me and said that she would be there if I ever needed her, to stand up for myself and to not allow Stephen to do this again. If he did, I must leave the relationship immediately. I agreed to do so if need be.

I had a long talk with Stephen's mother about what had happened and told her the situation. I knew that I would have her support if I needed it.

I decided that I could trust him and knew that if I had to end the marriage one day due to violence I could! I cried as I walked down the aisle on our wedding day, thinking, *What if this happens again?* They were tears of excitement and fear all at the same time.

I am not condoning abuse of any type, nor do I think that women or men should stay in marriages that are abusive. For me I knew that this was a lesson to stand up for myself and show him that I was in charge of me.

I am happy to say that we have been married for fifteen years and that there has never been another incident of physical abuse. There have been many ups and downs, as there are in most marriages, but I have always stood in my power since that day.

I have been working with Aphrodite for quite a few years now to reopen the passion in my sacral chakra, to view my sexuality as a celebration, and to not feel shameful about my body. I have worked very hard to heal these events in my lifetime and feel that this book is the final chapter in healing those events for myself.

I invite Aphrodite into my life to help me feel at ease with my body and my thoughts. She has been by my side giving me the confidence to trust in men.

I am even treating male clients now in my crystal healing practice, when I once vowed I was only here on Earth to help women heal!

So take some time right now to invite Aphrodite into your life to help balance your sacral chakra and enable your true passion and creativity to flow throughout radiating your true essence.

Crystal Healing

You may wish to place the raw blue aquamarine on your throat chakra to assist in any deep emotional healing that needs to be cleansed from your throat chakra. Aquamarine was believed to be a treasure of mermaids in ancient times bringing forth good luck and protection. Aquamarine is a water element stone that connects you to the divine feminine, freeing you of attachments to old patterns, relationships and ways of being. Remember the universe will always create that which is for your highest good if you allow it!

Affirmation

Here is a little invocation that you can use to call Aphrodite:

"Sister Aphrodite, I invite you into my space to help heal any issues that I may have that could be affecting my sacral chakra in a negative way. Please assist me in balancing the yin and yang within my soul."

Dedication

I would like to dedicate this chapter to my oldest daughter Kayla Dawn Silver Hughes.

Chapter 18

Bast

Independence

Color: Gold
Crystal: Brown or Red Tiger's Eye

Bast is the bold goddess of strength, independence, and wisdom. She strives to forge forward and overcome any and all obstacles that she may encounter on her path of her true-life purpose. Bast was an Egyptian goddess serving other women in ancient times. She changed her life purpose of being a servant to a future of having her own servants and expanding her power into an independent, strong feminine role. Bast if often depicted as a feline creature of grace and infinite knowledge. She walks tall, with confidence, a bit of sass, and has a very deep knowing of all things.

> It is important as a woman that we maintain the traits of wisdom, grace, independence, and still honor our inner child with play.

She wants to share with all of us those qualities of how to walk fearlessly through life. Do not fear being alone but know that all divine things come from taking that very time alone each and every day to hear our truest feminine thoughts. Hear your sacred soul speak to you at a very deep level and fill your soul with those very creative vibrations of knowing on all levels of your physical, emotional, and spiritual being on this planet Mother Earth.

We as women need to ground our feet to Mother Earth so that we have the confidence and knowledge to walk our talk and truly be who we are to be. Do not put on a facade of someone that we think that we need to be on this planet. What is your biggest dream? Have you ever been strong enough to watch the movie of who you really are? Let your ego sleep while you dream this incredible film about you?

As a woman, we tend to be the eyes for our loved ones and families watching over them and tending to their needs.

It is vital to honor our independence and allow our wings to spread and to fly freely in balance in a committed relationship. Many times we may tend to find comfort in the union of marriage, having our partner do many things that we were once capable of doing. You might find it easier for your husband/partner to do these tasks for you.

In Egyptian times, there were some very honored women as in many lifetimes before. But over the last few centuries woman's role has diminished in many cultures. In some, women aren't honored in public at all. This energy has affected the feminine energy within the universe and it is time to help bring forth that loving feminine energy to flow harmoniously with the masculine energy to maintain Gaia's loving union.

> *I, Bast, am willing to help women with this characteristic and need, if one if ready to take that next step on their life path. If you feel that you are ready to step forth onto your life path, and you feel that you don't have the courage to be independent, then ask me to assist you with this and I will. Talk to me during your daily meditation, tell me your deepest fears, and I can hold your hand and walk you through these challenges as they arise. I will surround you with my strong, feminine, graceful energy, holding you in that place of courage and independence until you are ready to fly your own.*

My energy is very much like a cat. I am fiercely independent, and I am not afraid to walk alone on the physical plane knowing that I am securely supported by strong loving divine beings aiding me along my path. When you are physically walking alone on this Earth, ask for support and you can build your own spiritual team to assist you with all of your needs. If you are planning a healing retreat, I can assist you by providing marketing tools, a course outline, and locations with good energy for the event, and I will help attract attendees that will benefit from your workshop. All you need to do is ask me to be here.

Bast has a very wise nature about her. She uses her feminine intuition and honors herself fully. She knows that we each have our own wisdom that will always allow us to move forth on a path of love and light honoring our soul's purpose. When you have a question in life, ask your higher self and then trust in the answer, even if it is completely different from what others are telling you.

My example of this happened recently. I was very ill with an ear infection in both ears, my throat, and my sinuses. I was subsequently put on very strong antibiotics for ten days to clear all of the infections. I noticed about seven days into the course of the antibiotics that I had spiking fevers and that my facial/head pain was a 10/10. I was sleeping with an ice pack on my face and taking pain analgesics to try to get the pain under control. At one point, I told my husband that if I had a gun I would be done, as I had never experienced this type of uncontrollable pain before. I know that I have a fairly high pain tolerance as I had two of my daughters without an epidural.

My intuition told me to watch a TV show that day, and sure enough I had the symptoms of post-herpetic trigeminal neuralgia affecting the fifth cranial nerve in my head. This can happen when you don't get an antiviral prescription when you have shingles, which I had had six months earlier.

I went to my physician and told her that this is what I thought was happening to my physical body and she agreed. She told me that I should go on a cycle of anticonvulsants so that my neurons won't continue to send pain signals after the nerve inflammation has settled down. I was scared at first thinking, *Okay, if I don't do this I will suffer for the rest of my life in pain.* Then I had a friend help me tap into what really was the root cause of these physical manifestations. I knew that I was going through a huge transformation, truly stepping into my feminine power of teaching and leading many women through transformations in this lifetime as I had in many lifetimes before.

I intuitively got the message that there was a serpent that had been lying dormant on the right side of my brain, exactly where the cranial nerve was showing the signs of inflammation. I talked to the serpent and asked it to move down throughout my spinal column and move this ancient energy through this structure. I had placed this serpent there to keep myself safe from the ancient knowledge that I knew from all of those lifetimes before, and to keep myself from being executed for my strength and wisdom as a feminine being.

I knew that this was going to be a long process but I also trusted in the goddesses that they wouldn't give me anything that I couldn't handle.

I have a fair amount of medical knowledge from my career of working in hospitals in this lifetime, along with being a doctor in past lifetimes, so I had to really keep putting this knowledge to the side, knowing that I needed to treat this transformation with spiritual integrity and trust, trust, trust.

I had decided to try the anticonvulsants to help with the pain in my head, knowing that my body would tell me when it was time to go off them. Sure enough, twelve days into the anticonvulsants I had an extremely sore throat and a rash began to develop on both arms. I was very confused and unable to focus. I was guided to look at the drug sheet that showed me all of the allergic reactions to the drug and, yes, I had them all.

So off to the doctor I went and told her that I was having an allergic reaction. She told me that this anticonvulsant is used on a lot of people and that there have hardly been any allergic reactions reported. She wasn't sure that this was one. I knew it was, and after three days of discontinuing the medication the symptoms of my reaction subsided.

I am not encouraging you to avoid advice from a medical professional. I am just encouraging you to be the captain of your ship and use your intuitive wisdom to guide your health if need be. I trusted that my body would tell me when I could stop taking the medication, and it did very loudly! So listen to your physical body. It is a very wise vessel that houses our spirit.

When I tapped in again, I was told that I didn't need to be on any medications at all. When I go to Hawaii in a few weeks, I will complete this cycle of transformation and complete my healing process.

So yes, I completely trusted in the divine. I muscle-tested with the medication and was shown that my body didn't need it.

Our family had a trip planned to go to Kona, Hawaii, for two weeks. I knew once again that this trip was not only a holiday but also a deep healing to aid me in my life path.

As soon as we landed, I went straight to the ocean and swam in the blue magical waters, asking the sisters of the oceans and Mother Earth to help recycle this transformative energy that I was ready to release. I also dropped my roots deeply into the black lava rock, asking Pele to assist me with this reactivation to help harmonize this higher vibrating energy within my being. It was like a vacuum. I could feel her sucking the lower energy out of my feet from the residual symptoms of the virus.

I had also booked a private wild dolphin charter for my family and two other families to help with the energetic shifts that I needed to move through this transformative cycle. The dolphins will sonar your chakras and help you heal if you ask them. As soon as we saw the first pod of dolphins, I jumped in and started swimming by one old dolphin, asking him for some healing and shifting.

During this encounter, I had one of the dolphins play the leaf game with me. One carries a leaf on its nose or fin and then drops it in front of you for you to throw it. I was so excited that I forgot to take a photo. I was guided to bring the leaf home to put on my altar to remind me to trust that all things are possible.

So all in all, Bast is the intuitive goddess of grace, wisdom, and play. Don't be afraid to be independent, to be courageous, and to step out there. Know that you're never alone. Your spiritual support team won't ever let you down or won't complete their tasks. Allow your inner child to be fulfilled with playtime for yourself, friends, and family. You can have the balance of being powerful, independent, walking with grace, and able to play when warranted.

Crystal Healing

Please place the red or brown tiger's eye crystal on your solar plexus (belly button) chakra to help you balance your independence with the strength of Mother Earth and Father Sky. Pull the two connecting energies to your power center (solar plexus chakra). At this time, please think of the intention or goal that you are wanting to accomplish in your life at this moment and feel the power of your golden yellow solar plexus building and expanding, supporting your thoughts and goals. Each time you do this crystal healing, you may choose a different intention or build upon the same one until you reach your goal.

Affirmation

"You are a divine leader walking with your head held tall, a smile upon your face supported by the divine feminine and masculine creating the seeds of your dreams, nurturing them, then patiently waiting for them to bloom into your deepest dreams!"

Dedication

I would like to dedicate this chapter to Colleen Sinram, a woman who has all of the qualities of Bast and is very near to my heart!

Chapter 19

———⦿❀❀⦿———

Coventina

Nature

Color: Blue-Green
Crystal: Larimar

Coventina is a Celtic goddess who helps to purify our bodies
and minds if we ask her to. She watches over all of the bodies of
water on Mother Earth: the rivers, oceans, ponds, and streams.
She is the goddess who will help you eliminate toxins from your
body through the process of using water as a ritual. Coventina
strongly urges you to drink pure water to cleanse your cells
and body of any negative or lower energies that you may have
accumulated through your environment, the food you eat, or
what you drink.

> *You have the ability to purify your bodies to become
> clean vessels using the healing properties of water. Our
> physical bodies are largely composed of water. We need
> to feed our cells and organs with high vibrating water.
> Many of us don't even realize that we need water
> until our bodies are dehydrated and start to show us
> signs of dehydration, either through a headache or
> a dry mouth and lips. We need to listen to this finely
> tuned instrument that we call our body. We need to
> breathe more and drink more water, two key points to
> remember in your lifetime.*

I have been using guidance from Coventina for a few years now to purify my physical body with this magical fluid.

A few years ago, when I went to Kona, Hawaii, for a seminar, I was guided to spend as much time in the ocean as I could. As we were flying over the big blue ocean I could feel the dolphins, whales, and ocean inviting me to join them when I was ready. As soon as my plane landed I went to my hotel, put on my swimsuit, and headed straight for the beautiful aquamarine ocean. I could feel all of the heavy energy that I had picked up from other people's anxieties and fears about flying on the airplane as well as anger, resentment, and jealousy.

I purposefully walked toward the water asking Coventina to please accompany me while I was in the salty ocean water. I gave her permission to clear my auric field from all of the energy that was not mine. I was floating on my back, looking at Sister Sun and asking her also to join me in amplifying this cleansing and purification process.

I could feel Coventina's love as she joined in my own personal healing session in Mother Earth's womb, the magical ocean. I made sure that my hair was wet and cleansed as well as my body. I cupped the ocean water in my hand and bathed my third eye, clearing all negative and lower energies that I may have picked up along my journeys and lives.

I began to feel lighter as I was treading water in the healing water of the ocean. I felt like a mermaid spinning around in circles to the right and then switching and gently floating in a circle to the left, cleansing the energy of my auric field at a very deep level.

I would swim out into the open ocean where there was no one so that I could enjoy the solitude of my cleansing ritual! This is a gift that I give to myself each and every time I am near the ocean. My soul craves to be in the water or near it. I know that one day I will have a summer home that is near the water so that I may enjoy this natural cleansing ritual daily.

I realize that many of us don't live near an ocean, so I believe that another good alternative is to create your own Dead Sea salt bath every night. The goddesses have given me several different recipes to program Dead Sea salts with healing crystals to use in your own bath tub. I have created different sea salt mixtures to accompany each of my goddess meditations, each with a different intention.

It is very important that you clear your auric field each night with a Dead Sea salt bath. It works best if you can have the water as warm as you can stand with a couple of tablespoons of Dead Sea salt in the bathtub. You can also put a healing crystal in the bath, thinking what you're wanting to manifest during that cleansing ritual. A pink rose quartz is a good crystal to use in the bath as it will radiate love and healing in the water that envelops your physical body.

The Dead Sea salt will pull out any impurities that you may have picked up in your auric field. I am a strong believer that disease enters your body through the seven layers of your aura into your chakras. Keep your auric field clean and light. You can also have a shower if a bath isn't available and use the Dead Sea salt as a paste to rub on your body. This is a very useful tool to teach your children at a young age so they know the importance of keeping a clean aura.

In addition to the programmed Dead Sea salt recipes from the goddesses, they have also given me sacred recipes to create water elixirs that carry different intentions. I use water from our natural water well to create these healing elixirs. I was first guided by the goddess Isis to make an elixir to keep my goddess flame burning brightly within my solar plexus. She gave me the specific crystals to use in the water in conjunction with using the full moon's healing properties. I did exactly what I had been guided to do and after seven days of creating this healing elixir I tried my very first glass. I filled up an eight-ounce glass with Isis's healing elixir. As I was swallowing this water, I could feel my throat chakra starting to expand and flutter with a high vibrating energy. Then this energy flowed down into my heart and started swirling around and around in a clockwise direction. I could feel my heart chakra expanding. At this point, I was in awe of what was happening with my body and that this water really works. I took another large sip of the elixir and I could feel this energy move down into my solar plexus, warming this powerful energy center. I felt an immediate sense of peace in my power center. I could feel this yellow chakra expanding and letting go of all restrictions that I had felt in my stomach before taking a sip of this water. Then the energy moved down to my sacral chakra, and then finally to my red root chakra and down my legs into Mother Earth.

I knew what I had felt. But would others feel what I had? I patiently waited for my good friend Kathy to come for a visit, as she is also an intuitive with strong clairsentience so I knew that if anyone else was going to feel what I felt it would be her. I also knew that she would be honest with me and tell me if I was crazy! So, when she arrived, she said, "Please pour me a glass of this amazing elixir," and she giggled with excitement. I waited patiently as she took her first drink. Then her eyes got big and she said that she could feel this high vibrating energy circling around her heart chakra and releasing emotions that she had stored in that chakra. She said, "This elixir is amazing. Wow!" We both laughed and drank more elixir.

I have since made many more elixirs from secret recipes from different goddesses to heal many different needs. All of my clients and friends who use the goddess elixirs are very strong repeat customers. I can relate to this as my body now craves these healing waters. My two younger daughters love drinking the "moon" water, and I am so delighted that they have been introduced to the goddess energy at such a young age. They will not have to go through a lot of the lessons that I have because of this knowing beforehand.

As you can see, there are many ways to invite Coventina into your life to help you purify your auric field and physical body. You can use the natural earthly bodies of water if you have access to them or you can create your own body of cleansing and healing water in your very own bath!

Please ask Coventina to assist you with these purification rituals. She wants to help you.

Crystal Healing

For this crystal healing, you will want to hold the magic larimar in your left hand connecting to your past lifetimes related to water and let your magic work with it. Please place the blue crystal on your throat chakra to allow you to connect to the nurturing, feminine aspects of your being. Feel the gently flowing energy of this crystal soothing your throat and calming your mind, allowing you to cleanse your soul in nature. If you feel emotional after this crystal healing, allow your feelings to be released and nurtured by your divine Mother.

Affirmation

"Allow the energy in your body and aura to shine like the pure vibration of the molecules of water. You are the true essence of divine water. Feed this craving and it will fill your soul"

Dedication

I would like to dedicate this chapter to my wise friend Loretta Blume who has supported my work and has a huge heart.

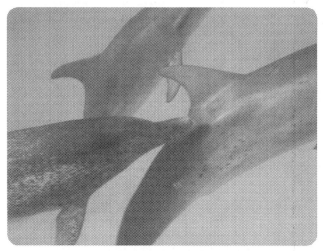

A photo I took while swimming in Kona, Hawaii, with the wild dolphins.

Chapter 20

Diana

Manifestation

Color: Yellow
Crystal: Golden Topaz

Diana is a moon goddess often depicted carrying a silver bow and arrow given to her by her father Jupiter. She is a Roman goddess with piercing blue eyes. She is associated with healthy child birthing because her mother gave birth to Diana and her twin brother effortlessly and without pain. She is connected to nature spirits and is strongly associated with oak trees. You can call upon Diana to help with healing all animals, to connect with elemental spirits, and to help you stay focused on your goals.

> *Please call upon me to help you prepare a schedule that will manifest your goals and intentions. I will help you create the space in your schedule to meet your priorities with efficiency and harmony. It is important to honor your goals, stay on track, and say "no" to others' demands on your time. The effort that you put forth to achieve your intentions and goals will fulfill your soul with a life force energy of peace and empowerment. I will help you stay focused on your end product and attain a sense of balance in your life.*

Diana is a very wise goddess who has helped me complete this book. I have felt her very strong loving presence around me for the three years that it has taken me to channel this book and my healing meditations.

It was two years ago that I was intuitively guided to channel my first healing meditation with the goddess Isis. I remember thinking, *What am I doing channeling these words from the goddesses? Who is going to listen to these meditations and what if they think that I am crazy because I can communicate with the goddesses?* I had a lot of fear-based thoughts like these running through my mind. But, before I knew it, I was in Kona, Hawaii, and recording my first meditation CD with Mark Watson at Angel Earth Recording Studio.

I had met Mark during a course I attended on the Big Island of Hawaii many months before recording the CD. I felt a very sure sense that I was to record a series of channeled healing meditations from many goddesses and to include a programmed crystal healing kit to go with the meditations. I knew that we used to chant healing words while using crystals in many past lives as healers, and that this wisdom should be brought forth to help empower and heal all of us on Earth now.

My voice was very shaky during the recording of the Isis meditation. We tried many different things to soothe my throat, but deep down I knew that nothing would change the vibration of my voice during that recording. It was something that I needed to release regarding my fear of being powerful and teaching others in this lifetime. I know that I have had many lifetimes of teaching others and have been killed many times before for doing so. I have had neck troubles in the past, whiplash many times, and scarring in my neck. I know that these conditions all were calls to heal my throat chakra.

My spirit guides told me that my voice needed to be in that vibration during the Isis and Dana meditations. Those vibrations would help others in a way that would bring up energies that needed to be released, to the top of the chakra, and they could then flow out of the chakra. I had done this as a healer in a past life. I needed to stop worrying about my voice as I was being used as a divine channel for others to heal.

I have now channeled and created nine healing meditations from different goddesses. The crystal healing kits are programmed by the goddesses and the divine to amplify the meditation process. I have felt Diana's strong presence gently, but firmly, pushing me to reach my goals and work through any fears that come up when I am channeling these ancient words of wisdom and healing.

I know that that these healing meditations are truly channeled words for me to first heal myself and then share with others who may have the same wounds as I have had in my lifetime and in past lifetimes. The feminine energy is gently awakening within Mother Earth and the ancient feminine wisdom from the past is being brought forward to the present and the future. I know that I have agreed to come back to help Mother Earth and the feminine energy fulfill the transformations and goals that were set in sacred contracts years and years ago.

You must know that when I started channeling this ancient wisdom that I had concerns about what others would think. I even wondered if I was crazy at first, but, now through much experience and clarity, I know that I am on the right path and that I am fulfilling my manifested intentions with passion, joy, and love. Bringing this wisdom into words for other souls to heal and to empower their lives, and help them move forward with their life purpose is what I am doing.

I have felt such a sense of peace and joy within my heart, knowing that I am surrounded by divine protection and love. It is time for each of us to be brave and bring forth our ancient wisdom and to look deep within our souls and heal the wounds that we are ready to see. Please trust that Diana will be with you every step of the way. She will help you see yourself like an ancient oak tree, your feet grounded firmly and safely in Mother Earth's soil being fertilized by her love, while allowing your ideas to grow like tree branches, expanding and being nurtured by Father Sky, Sister Sun, and Sister Moon. Trust that we are one with spirit and that we can manifest our goals and intentions with the loving infinite support of Mother Earth and all beings of love and light.

Crystal Healing

You may wish to hold the golden topaz up to your third eye and feel your loving intention that you are wishing to manifest emanate out of your third eye into the matrix of the crystal. When you are guided to, please place the golden topaz on your solar plexus chakra. Feel the energy of the crystal opening your solar plexus and filling it with golden rays from the sun. See this chakra expanding and filling with loving manifestation energy.

Affirmation

"Trust that your intuition will guide you down the road. Allow your higher self to guide you with divine ideas to help manifest the goals that you are wishing to attain."

Dedication

I would like to dedicate this chapter to my sister goddess Chantelle Klein who carry many qualities of Diana throughout all that she has been through.

Chapter 21

———— ❧ ————

Eireen

Honoring the Inner Child

Color: Light Pink
Crystal: Labradorite, Rhodochrosite

Eireen is the Greek goddess of peace, justice and fairness. She is there to help celebrate and honor the inner child within each and every one of us. Eireen can be depicted holding a small child in her arms with her long black wavy hair topped off with a tiara made of white seashells and pearls to complement her white linen gown trimmed with soft white lace.

What exactly does the term *inner child* mean?

Each one of us is believed to have an inner child within our soul, and it honors our child-like qualities of joy, belief, play, friendship, loving without restrictions and complete and total trust in life itself.

Eireen is a goddess who can help you bring back some of the childlike qualities that our energy fields need to remain balanced and healthy. Most often in this world today we put on our professional *suits* five days a week, and for some it could be seven days a week. Our lives are controlled by schedules filled with meetings, appointments and very tightly time-controlled schedules. We have forgotten that there are days that we need to connect with Mother Earth. Go outside and lie down on the green grass or lie in the snow and make a snow angel, or look up at the clouds and see what shapes the white billowy clouds are making. Our soul craves for this *free* time in our lives. Honoring yourself enough to put some play time in your schedule will go a long way in aiding you to maintain a healthy life physically, energetically and spiritually.

Eireen strongly urges you to try this for a week. Plan some free time in your day timer and see what happens. Your mind may find this quite incomprehensible and you may find yourself wondering what you're going to do with that free time. You may draw a blank, as that is what happens when you forget to honor your inner child and feel peace within your soul.

Do something easy. Go for a walk in the park, swing on the swings, walk through a flower garden, smell the scents and even pick some flowers that you find beautiful.

You may wish to simply go outside on a piece of green grass, lie down and watch the clouds move by, changing shape and continuing on their way. You may wish to blow bubbles in your backyard. Another idea might be Hula-Hooping. Don't laugh at this idea. I took a hula-hooping course while attending a women's weekend retreat. I thought that it would be fun to Hula-Hoop, something that I had not tried since I was in grade-twelve physical education. I walked into a room with my good friend Karen and saw a very fit, bubbly woman and about twenty brightly colored hula-hoops lying on the floor. She welcomed us to her Hula-Hooping class and asked us to go ahead and pick out our favorite Hula-Hoop. My inner child kicked in and said, "Yeah, look at all of the brightly colored hoops." This instructor makes her own Hula-Hoops from black tubing and then puts iridescent, brightly colored tape around the hoop. I picked a purple hoop that was wrapped with rainbow-colored metallic tape, shimmering with all the colors of the rainbow! She asked us all when the last time we had hula-hooped was. As for most women, it had been at least fifteen to twenty years.

She started the music, which was very hip-hop, and told us to put the hoops on our hips and begin to rotate our hips slowly to the right. I was having great success and fun rotating the Hula-Hoop around and around my midsection! Then she asked us to move the hoop up and down our torso by using the speed of our body movement. That was successful, but then she asked us to move the hoop up our body to our neck and then use one of our arms to move the hoop onto our hands and twirl the hoop between our fingers! My head was saying, "Yeah right," and my inner child was loudly yelling, "Yeah that sounds fun, let's do it." So over and over I kept trying, and then I finally accomplished the task.

After twenty minutes of the hooping, I started to feel intense pain around my ribs and hips. Every time the hoop would hit either one of these tender spots, I would grit my teeth. I thought, *I don't remember feeling this pain when I was a child."* Soon enough, most of the women in the group were feeling this pain. The instructor said, "Don't worry. If you keep this up, you won't have this pain."

At the end of the sixty-minute class, she offered many of these brightly colored hoops for sale. Once again my inner child spoke loudly, telling me to buy the brightest one: "Get the purple one with the hot pink metallic tape!" So I did.

Of note, the next day I was bruised from my ribs down to my hips, completely black, hot to touch and very tender! This made me laugh thinking, *Even though my heart-inner child is still a seven-year-old girl, my physical body may feel something different!*

That story is just a reminder how we can honor our inner child to allow our mind and body to feel inner peace and tranquility. We need to remember that we can't keep putting off today, thinking that we can do it tomorrow. We need to truly honor our inner child with love and nurturing, which will allow us to radiate peace and love, which will bring harmony to all aspects of our being. We are one with nature and we need to connect with her to keep our bodies healthy and alive.

Eireen wants you to know that you can ask her to help you when you are in a situation that you feel is lacking equality or fairness. She is a gentle energy that will support you and give you ideas of what you might say or do to bring more harmony to the situation. She will allow you to see through her eyes. You may view the situation as a lesson to become a better person on this earthly plane. Sometimes when we are given really hard lessons we get stuck in a place of grief and pain. We can't seem to turn the box around and see the gift inside that we have been asking for from the divine. If you can remember, when you're in those times of despair, open up your chakras and connect with the divine. Ask Eireen what the blessing of this situation is for you. What is the gift that the divine sends you?

Be patient, breathing deeply and listening to what answers she has for you. Remember the divine doesn't see time as we do. Be patient. Your version of how much time you have allotted for an answer may be part of the lesson and you will receive your guidance in divine timing. This is hard for us who are an Aries astrological sign and have a hard time being patient! Practice makes perfect. That is my motto during those times.

Crystal Healing

For this crystal healing please, place the labradorite crystal on your third eye to bring forth the magic divine play that will help spark the creative energy that your soul is craving. The labradorite crystal reminds us that magic is at play in your daily life. Allow the magic of this crystal to lead you to your shimmering dreams.

You may also use the pink rhodochrosite crystal, which represents the inner child on your heart chakra. If you feel like you have lost touch with the child-like qualities in yourself, please ask this crystal to help rejuvenate those carefree, spontaneous moments in your daily life.

Affirmation

"Dear ones, honoring the childlike qualities, fairness, and trust are some of the hardest traits to practice, but I do ask that you try as it will bring many blessings into your life."

Dedication

I would like to dedicate this chapter to my aunt, Gloria Noble, who honors her inner child.

Here I am Hula-Hooping!

Chapter 22

Hathor

Receiving

Color: Burgundy
Crystal: Red Sedona Rock

Hathor is an Egyptian goddess who is depicted having cow's horns holding a sun disc in the center. Hathor is the goddess who personifies beauty, love, music, motherhood, childbirth, and joy. She is a very important deity throughout the history of Egypt. She also plays the role of a sky goddess and a sun goddess with the god Ra.

Geometric patterns are the quilted network that house the universe with life force. If you look around, you will see different geometric symbols everywhere in the world, seen and unseen with our physical eyes. Many circles create the flower of life, a universal symbol that we are divinely connected as one. The circle represents no beginning and no ending, just a continuous circle of love and light. The sun is a perfect circle, changing colors as it needs to. The moon changes shape to help shed light in different patterns on Mother Earth that shift with the universal flow of life. Mother Earth is a circle symbolizing the continuous infinite embodiment of life-force energy encompassing all that is. The circle plays a very important role in our energy system. There are many different shapes in our sky represented by the constellations and the night stars. The glowing stars of the night sky symbolize the importance of shining light from all aspects of our light bodies and emanate light to all. Now is the time to awaken our ancient knowledge that we have had in past lifetimes to connect our energy to shapes within our physical bodies to universal bodies and unseen energies merging our energies as one life force.

I had planned a trip for Stephen and me to stay at a resort in Sedona, Arizona, for a few days in December 2010. I had been to this resort before so I knew exactly where I wanted to go hiking. I needed to connect with the goddess Hathor while I was hiking in the Boynton Canyon. We left early in the morning and began to hike up the red rock trail toward the Kachina Woman rock formation.

I knew that Hathor was beside me as I was walking up the path toward this rock formation. She was asking me to practice the art of receiving today. As I was hiking up the trail, I was looking to find an area around Kachina Woman where there were other people. I heard Kachina Woman ask me to pick up seven red rocks along my path to use for my healing sessions on my clients and to remain connected to her. I love picking rocks, so this was a very exciting task for me. I found at least seven shiny red rocks in all sizes and shapes as she had requested. My pockets were heavy with these divine formations. I sat down with my back against Kachina Woman and I immediately asked for her permission to be there and to receive healing from her. I heard her say, "Dear one, yes you may receive healing from me. Please tell me exactly where you wish to receive this healing energy in your body." She also said, "I am grateful that you are here to receive healing for yourself as I know you will share this high energy vibration with others in your life and work."

I told her that I would like to receive healing in my lungs to help my asthma. I also asked that I might receive healing in my neck as I have a lot of scar tissue in my cervical spine and thoracic spine. I asked that it all be regenerated to its perfect healthy condition. I thanked her for this healing and time alone with her. As I sat with my back against her beautiful red body, with the sun shining on my face, I could feel her energy come up through my feet and into my solar plexus and heart chakras. The palms of my hands were gently facing palm down on the red surface and I began to feel the energy running up my arms into my heart. Then I heard her say, "Lean back into me as I will support you. Allow your back to be supported by my structure." So I leaned back onto her body and I could feel this pain in the back of my heart chakra. I started to breathe very slowly and deeply, giving permission to release anything of a lower vibration out of my back into Mother Earth.

Next she guided me to allow my head to rest on her formation. I could feel the back of my head, at my third eye, start to ache. I knew that my body was now releasing and letting go of lessons that I had learned. I saw my spirit leave my body as Kachina Woman asked if she could do a spiritual ceremony with me. I agreed with honor and gratitude. I could see her lie my spiritual body down on her red rock, and in a clockwise rotation she placed sage around my body in a circle. She then ceremoniously lit each sage bundle one at a time, starting at the one o'clock position. She sang a native chant as she lit these bundles of this sacred plant. She then placed native arrows on my spiritual body to make the shape of a star. She asked if I wished to receive the activation of my life as a medicine woman from one of my past lives. I was very honored and agreed. She said that she would do this activation in exchange for using these ancient healing tools in my healing with my clients.

Kachina Woman sang a chant all in her native tongue. It was a beautiful song and I could feel my heart chakra opening up and attuning to this ancient healing vibration. Kachina Woman thanked me for being willing to share my healing words and wisdom with others on Earth. I thanked Kachina Woman at the end of the ceremony and left her an offering. She strongly urged me to hike to one of the highest platforms of her rock formation and to bring my red rocks. I hesitated for a moment when I saw how high this was, but then trusted that I would be okay. I slowly moved forth on the path to the top of the rock platform. When I reached the top, I heard her ask me to place the red rocks in a cave enclosure near the base of her, in a circle formation. I did this and then listened for her next guidance. She then asked me to place one hand on her large wall and the other over the circle of red rocks. I could feel her energy flowing through my body into the red rocks that I had placed in the circle. She then blessed the rocks and we closed the ceremony.

I sat there in a moment of bliss and wondered if this had really taken place. My physical body felt very light and my mind was feeling quite disoriented. I slowly gathered up my rocks, thanking Kachina Woman and Hathor for this amazing morning activation.

I normally don't take rocks from a location unless I am strongly guided to do so, as I believe that they should be left in their original environment. In this situation, Kachina Woman strongly guided to me use her red rocks for healing purposes to help the world but to bring them back to her home when I returned in a few months.

As you can see, Hathor is a very strong advocate for us to practice the art of receiving. Receiving strengthens the feminine side of our bodies as giving enforces the masculine. When we balance these actions, the energy can flow evenly throughout our physical body, maintaining our health.

Crystal Healing

If you ever get the chance to sit in a vortex in Sedona on the red rock, I ask that you do it. Being in a vortex will bring forth the issues that you need to heal in your life and will assist in healing those deep wounds.

Place the red rock on your heart chakra or in the palm of your left hand to receive the loving vibration and wisdom of this magical red rock. Breathe deeply and feel the love that these beautiful red stones carry from years of experience and wisdom.

Affirmation

"Please consider receiving as honorable as giving. We must have harmony within our bodies to maintain a healthy body."

Dedication

I would like to dedicate this chapter to Kachina Woman.

A photo I took of Kachina Woman in Boynton Canyon, Sedona, Arizona.

Chapter 23

—∘⊰❀⊱∘—

Ishtar

Peace & Honor

Color: Ruby Red
Crystal: Ruby

Ishtar is a Babylonian goddess who was invoked in ancient times to help with fertility, sexuality, nurturing, protection, and knowledge. Her energy is the essence of Venus's feminine energy. She is a very strong feminine goddess but has many qualities that one can call upon for needs that one might have. In ancient Babylonian times, Ishtar would carve out time to honor her divine connection first thing in the morning and then last thing before shutting her eyes at night. This practice will strongly benefit those who use it in today's culture.

One of the hardest life lessons that we learn while in our physical bodies upon Earth is to honor our spirit and body first and foremost before giving and pleasing others. We are born a true spirit of our creator and then slowly learn our physical human ways by detaching from our creator and being our own individual person. We learn that the human way is to please others first and make others happy, forgetting that we should not feel guilty for nurturing our souls first and fill up our cup as a priority. A soul can't reach its full potential when half empty, for we are created to fill our body with light daily and hourly if need be. Please make

yourself a priority every day by nurturing your soul to
feel peace deep within while honoring your spirit.

Boundaries can sometimes be a dirty word to some people. Some of us have too many and some have none at all. We have come here on Earth to obtain a happy medium: receiving and giving in equal parts. This can be tied to the obligation vibration that I have talked about in previous chapters in this book.

Boundaries are actually a very healthy energetic blue print to have so that you can accomplish the goals and dreams of your life. Some areas that you may wish to have specific boundaries are in your career life, your relationships with your spouse and friends, your children, your parents, your physical body, eating, and for any addictions you might have. Having self-nurturing boundaries allows us to set the bar of honor for our soul while feeling the peace within.

I had to set some tight guidelines and boundaries while I was writing this book. I knew that I wanted to share the wisdom from the goddesses in written words as well as spoken guided healing meditations. I started off being intuitively guided from the goddess Isis, with her gently nudging me to write an outline for my book and asking which goddesses wished to share their wisdom. As you can imagine, I had a lot of negative mind chatter about writing my first book. I needed to have boundaries. I needed to tune out those negative thoughts by asking the divine and the goddesses to help me quiet their sound by making the divine words louder than the negative chatter. I also asked to receive an abundance of support from the goddesses in all ways; time to write the book, easy flow of words to type, support from the close friends keeping me on track while writing, and finally financial support to publish the book, all of which would give me inner tranquility.

I have been a people pleaser in my past, always wanting to make others happy, thinking of everyone else and not myself. I am a mother of three daughters, a wife to a cattle rancher, a gardener in the summer—mowing what feels like five hundred acres of lawn and planting hundreds of perennials to watch them bloom for three months of the year—and an accountant for our ranch. I have organized the girls' photo albums since birth, remembered everyone's birthday and anniversaries within both families, attended school functions, and helped start a new 4-H Beef Club for the youth in our community. Exhausting, isn't it, when you think of what you might do in one day let alone your lifetime here on Earth? If you were to add up the time that you have spent giving to others, some out of love and some out of obligation, do you think it would outweigh the time that you have truly allowed yourself to receive and nurture your soul?

I feel that we learn very quickly along the way what we want to do in life, and what we don't, and what we won't put up with. That learning accelerates in a relationship or marriage.

When I first met Stephen, I was working at the hospital, as I had been for ten years. I was very independent, had my own income and a very tight social knit group of people that I worked with. I was accepted in a bachelor of nursing program at a college that was three hours away. Stephen and I met in January of 1995, and I was to start college in September of that year in a program that was four years in length. I knew that I was going to make a decision that would alter my life path, but I was in love and that was my priority.

I made the decision to withdraw from the course and continued working at the hospital. Stephen and I were engaged in October 1995 and decided to get married on January 20, 1996.

On May 27, 1997, I gave birth to our first daughter: Kayla Dawn Silver Hughes. When I look back at my time of being pregnant with her, I see now that I would do things differently if I had only known how. I worked full-time until I was eight months pregnant. I had gained a whopping sixty pounds during the nine months of being pregnant. I was scared about being a mother for the first time and wondered if I would be any good at raising children. I was afraid to go through labor as I was adopted and didn't know any medical history about my own birth mother's labor with me. I realized that I had no boundaries for food or loving myself. I wasn't feeling any peace in my soul, nor was I respecting myself. I was trying to fill those voids with ice cream and homemade pizza. I was very independent and it was hard for me to ask for help.

My motto was, "I will try to do it myself one, two or three times and then I might consider asking others to help me!" I remember I was nesting and was about two weeks before my due date. I decided that I was going to put up a new wallpaper border around our living room and kitchen walls by myself. If you can imagine this sight, I have a very huge belly and I fill up my wallpaper tray with water and I put the entire forty-foot roll of wallpaper border through the tray at once. I thought that would be easier than cutting and pasting the roll.

As I am standing on a step stool, I have a meter stick in my hand to help smooth down the paper as I start to put up the roll from one end of the living room. I am slowly moving my step stool and the meter stick rolling the wall border along the top of the ceiling. Then when I have about half of the wall border up, the initial placement of the wallpaper starts to slide down the wall very slowly and then it curls off the wall. I can feel the sciatic nerve in my buttocks screaming in pain as is my neck from looking up, but I am determined to do this project myself. Well, I am happy to say that I did accomplish this task myself but not without painful side effects. I could hardly move from the intense sciatic pain in my low back and buttocks until I gave birth to Kayla.

Now I laugh to myself as I realize nine years later that sciatic pain represents being hypocritical. That is exactly what I was doing and had done so many times in the past. I should have let go of my self-limiting belief that I am stronger when I do things on my own and that it is more of a nuisance to ask others to assist me.

I realize now that I should have been taking extra time to love and nurture myself during those times of being pregnant. It is not selfish to take a nap when you're pregnant, put your feet up and read a good book, and say "no" to others' demands.

Honoring your body as a temple is very important and even more so when you're carrying another life inside of you.

When I was pregnant with Josie, our second daughter, I did learn to take care of my physical body and that the extra weight wouldn't just fall off after I gave birth to her, like I thought it would when I had Kayla. I did commit to exercising daily doing step aerobics and walking, up until two weeks before giving birth. My physical body recovered from delivery a lot faster, despite having a broken tailbone because she was a large baby. I must say I was thankful to ground the energy daily into Mother Earth and keep the divine energy flowing through my body in a harmonious way.

Every year in late June, after the cows have their calves, we do a branding. This is an old cowboy tradition where you ride horses to round up the calves and cows. You separate the calves into their own pen, vaccinate them for certain viruses, and brand them with your ranch brand so they can be identified. We usually have about fifty people consisting of family, friends and neighbors who come and help for the celebratory day.

Some ranches are more old fashioned and traditional than others. The women do the cooking and the men are in the corral dealing with the cattle. As you can imagine, I don't like to be labeled nor do I usually fit into patriarchal paradigms. So when I came along I did help my mother-in-law Barb with the cooking but also wanted to be in the corral helping with the cattle, enjoying the sunshine and conversation.

Eventually, Stephen and I would have the branding meal at our home after the day was done. I do enjoy cooking and making new recipes, so I loved to try new foods and would plan a themed menu for the branding meal. Every year I would love to hear the feedback of what the crew thought of my different themes, and yes it was a success. In June 2000, I was pregnant with our third daughter Erin Rachel. My due date was at the end of July 2000. We had organized our branding for mid-June and I was doing the cooking along with Barb. I had two little toddlers on the go, at the time was working as an independent senior sales director with a home-based cosmetic company, and running a household. I was determined that I could be superwoman and do it all. I was going to keep up my sales production for my business, which meant filling customers' orders, attending the sales director week in San Antonio, and planning monthly team meetings.

About a week before the branding, I started to feel really tired and thought that I had a very bad cold. When I coughed, I had to brace my pregnant belly with a pillow as the pain was so intense. I knew that I had a fever but I didn't want to take any drugs being pregnant. My goal was to get through making the branding meal and then I would deal with my body. On the day of the branding, I was very ill and my massage therapist Tracy suggested that I had more than a cold, possibly pneumonia. So the next day after the branding I went to the doctor and he confirmed that I had pneumonia and had strained a muscle in my abdomen from coughing. I felt like my body was a wreck.

So why did I let my cup empty to the bottom? What was I thinking being pregnant and a martyr? What a great combination! I know that we do better when we know better and that is my advice to any woman who is pregnant: don't worry about pleasing others, take time for napping, reading a good book, meditating and eating healthy food for you and your baby.

I will be forty years old when this book is published in 2011. I feel that I have learned a lot about myself in the past fifteen years being a wife and mother. I now will take time each day to honor myself spiritually by meditating at least thirty to forty minutes. I take a few minutes in the morning to connect with the divine so that my day will be in flow with the universe and then a few minutes each night to reflect on my day. I also take a Dead Sea salt bath every night to clear my auric field of any negative or lower energies that I may have picked up during the day.

I also honor my body by doing thirty minutes of movement daily, whether it is walking outside or on my treadmill while listening to my goddess tunes or watching Oprah, the most amazing mentor a woman could ask for! I am balancing my *me* time in addition to my family time, my career, rest, and play.

It is vital that we honor ourselves first and take time out of our busy lives to connect with the divine source, and then all else will be at peace within our lives. I know that when I take time to use my healing crystals on my chakras, meditate, exercise, connect with my good friends, and spend quality time with my husband and family that I feel a sense of inner tranquility and peace in my heart. It does really all fall into place when you start your day off with boundaries and honoring yourself. Then the peace will be the miraculous outcome of your efforts.

Crystal Healing

Please place a red ruby crystal upon your root chakra to connect and ground your energy into the life force of Mother Earth. The ruby crystal will open up any blocks at the base of the spine to allow the kundalini (coiled energy) to rise up the spinal column like a serpent and allow the energy to flow up and out of the crown chakra. If you start to feel depressed and isolated, this is a symptom that your root chakra isn't connected with Mother Earth. Placing a ruby crystal on your root chakra and visualizing your roots extending down into her core will regenerate the vital life force and support of Mother Earth.

Affirmation

"You are worth creating boundaries for in your life. You are a divine soul that craves spiritual connection and reflective time. Honor this and you will receive many infinite gifts and blessings."

Dedication

I would like to dedicate this chapter to my goddess friend Tracy Waddell.

Chapter 24

———o◦ß◦o———

Isolt

Infinite Self-Love

Color: Ocean Blue
Crystal: Turquoise

Isolt is a Celtic goddess who was caught in a love triangle between her husband King Marc and her lover Sir Tristan. She is associated with true undying eternal love for yourself that can be amplified when you are outdoors in nature among the tree and flower spirits. She can also help you connect with any deceased loved ones whom you are wishing to communicate with.

Take a minute to lay your head upon the green blanket of grass, smell the flowers that are outside, and allow your gaze to drift upon the beautiful blue skies. Please go outdoors and lie down on the grass like you did as a child and ask me to connect you to your infinite loving self, to the self that will honor you in all ways. I can also help you speak with your departed loved ones either through thought or by writing a letter to them, asking your questions, and then I will assist you in channeling their messages for you. I am infinite true love and would be honored to assist you in healing your heart from any past wounds in this lifetime or past lifetimes, allowing your heart chakra to expand and flourish into the infinite being that you already are.

Our heart chakra is a vital energy center that naturally closes down when it is wounded. Many of us receive wounds through the many different experiences in our lifetime from birth until death. If our heart chakra becomes clogged with scars from our wounds, then this energy center can't flow properly and you will develop a disease associated with the organs and systems that are in the chest area, arms and hands.

If you can imagine a beautiful pink rose before it opens, the petals are closed tightly around the center of the flower. You may not even be able to smell the beautiful aroma of the rose until the petals slowly start to open from the outside in, being nourished with sunlight, water, and pure joy. We all enjoy the wonderful scent of a pink rose—such a healing scent.

When I took my aromatherapy course, I learned that it takes about thirty roses to make a drop of absolute rose oil, and about sixty thousand roses to make one ounce, and this is why true absolute rose oil is so expensive. The rose oil has over twenty-two healing properties that it can be used for. One symptom that it can be used for is heart palpitations, which is an irregular beating of the heart. So if you combine the aromatherapy knowledge with the function of the heart chakra, you can see that the heart is much like a rose itself.

We need to nurture our soul, which resides in our heart, with sunshine, love, water, and joy. It is important that we take time to release any negative wounds and emotions that might be stored in this chakra from past relationships and thoughts. One can do this releasing by doing regular energy healing sessions, through crystal healing, reiki sessions, hands-on healing techniques, and asking Isolt to help you to be aware of what lower energies you might have stored in your heart chakra that you might wish to bring up to the surface, acknowledge, release, and forgive, freeing this energy center from these lower energies that may eventually cause disease.

I believe that we will continually go through the process of releasing wounds from our hearts until we have the knowledge to protect and clear our auric fields continually. When I first started learning about the chakras and started to get healing sessions with reiki, crystal healing, cranio-sacral therapy, and doing guided meditations, I couldn't really sense energy moving through my physical body. After a few months of continual regular energy work on my body, I started to feel my chakras within my body.

I remember having a healing session with my friend Fawna and I started to feel a very intense sharp heart pain rotating in a clockwise direction within my heart. I told her about this pain and then I started to breathe deeply and asked for spiritual assistance with releasing this pain. I tapped into the pain and asked what it was representing. I heard, "If you are ready to let go of the pain in your heart that represented going through your adoption process, then give yourself permission to surrender and let go of this wound."

I thought that I had completely finished healing from being adopted as a baby when I channeled and recorded my compact disc meditation: *A Healing Meditation for Adopted Children with Mother Mary.* But then I heard, "Dear one, we release our wounds in layers and this will be the last of that wound. Breathe deeply and allow us to fill this wound with pink loving divine light. So I surrendered and allowed the pink light to gently fill my heart chakra and the intense pain completely dissipated. I could actually feel my heart chakra expand in my chest. This was a bit uncomfortable at first, as I could feel my lungs and stomach moving to accommodate this new energy within my heart chakra. I could feel the tears streaming down my face, feeling an immense sense of gratitude and love, truly surrendering and feeling the infinite love of my true essence!

This was the beginning of my clairsentience (intuitive empathy) on clear feeling truly awakening. It all started with my heart chakra clearing old wounds and energies that allowed the divine to flow in and expand this center. I felt so light and free and I felt love for myself for the first time in a very long time. I remember feeling this love for myself when I was about eight years old. This was the last time I had a recollection of feeling love in my heart. After our babysitter sexually molested me the next year, all I could feel was shame and guilt in my heart chakra. Then, as I didn't know how to clear my chakras, my energy field and chakras became clogged with negative and lower energies bringing on sickness and losing any clarity that I had with my decisions.

I feel very strongly about loving your heart chakra daily. I have already taught my three girls how to use a rose unconditional love essence on their heart chakra every morning. I use this roll-on essence as a divine tool to remind myself to look deep into my eyes, into my soul, and say "I love you, Velva Dawn," and I say this affirmation three times each morning.

At first it was very hard for me to look into my eyes and say these words, but now as my heart chakra is lighter I feel true love for myself. When I do my crystal healing sessions on clients, I always recommend this unconditional love essence for their heart chakra.

If your heart chakra is closed up and full of negative energy, you will have a hard time loving yourself and won't truly be able to love others with a high divine vibration. There will be strings attached to many of your actions and thoughts until you can clear the clutter from your heart center. You truly deserve to love yourself first, heal your heart, and then expand your love to others with a pure healthy vibration.

Many of us don't have these tools to help us along the way, so this is why I am sharing stories of how the divine, and the goddesses, have helped me heal my heart chakra.

Crystal Healing

If you wish to place a turquoise crystal upon your heart chakra or throat chakra for a few minutes each day, you will receive the vibration of wholeness from this healing crystal. The turquoise crystal will allow you to reflect upon the images within your soul that reside in your heart, allowing you to be aware of what it is that you may wish to heal at this time. Each time you do this healing session with this crystal, you may release a different wound. Remember that when we are aware of something that is when we are able to release it. Please give gratitude to the turquoise crystal for helping you facilitate these healings sessions.

Affirmation

"Your true essence is complete and the love that you have for yourself is infinite and abundant. Breathe in love and breathe out any negative thoughts that you are storing in your heart. You are love."

Dedication

I would like to dedicate this chapter to Nola Meston who is a radiant goddess soul.

A photo of a pink rose that I captured on my camera.

Chapter 25

Ixchel

Medicine Woman

Color: Olive Green
Crystal: Amazonite

The name *Ixchel* comes from the sixteenth-century name Aztec Earth goddess of midwifery and medicine in the Mayan culture. She is also known as the Grandmother; her two qualities are birthing and healing. Ixchel is known to have strong connections with the moon, being called the moon goddess, as the moon has associations with fertility and protection. She has also been perceived as a female warrior goddess with jaguar-like energy. She has a divine connection to control rain flow and the tides. She and her husband, the Sun God, gave life to many Mayan gods. Ixchel can also be called Lady Rainbow with her essence flowing through the fragments of water in a rainbow.

You are a natural powerful channel for divine healing using your own bag of sacred tools that you have acquired through learning many different healing modalities while here on Earth. You can bring forth ancient healing tools that you have kept in a sacred place within your soul to be used for your loving healing purposes in divine time. Don't be afraid of your natural healing power. Embrace this wisdom with love and confidence knowing that you are a physician

of the elements and the divine combining all of your
high vibrating energy wisdom within your soul.

Many of us are afraid to accept the true healing power that we are fully capable of. This may be due to our past lives and keeping sacred oaths that we took as higher priestesses, goddesses, gods, druids, magicians, wizards, countesses, counts, and all royal or sacred positions in those lifetimes. Many of us are just now awakening the true healing magic that we knew and used in many prior lifetimes.

I know that I have been killed many times for teaching my wisdom to others. I can recall some of those lifetimes, which have been very descriptive and painful. I know that I was burned at the stake in Salem, Massachusetts, during the Salem witch burnings. I have seen myself as a little girl thrown overboard on a pirate ship for being clairvoyant. I was killed in Avalon with a sword wound to my heart, and I saw my death during the fall of Atlantis. I have seen my death as an oracle in the Delphi caves in Athens, and many more.

I have been slowly activating and bringing forward my ancient healing tools and wisdom that I used in those lifetimes. I have been doing this by visiting spiritual sites around the world, being guided by the goddesses and the divine as to where I need to travel, with whom, and when.

Last July, I awoke one morning and kept hearing that I needed to go to Kona, Hawaii, to receive another activation and that I could record another goddess meditation while I was there. I heard the divine saying, "You need to go within four days. Check on the Internet, as there will be a good sale for your flight and hotel room." So still in my pajamas, I had my morning coffee and breakfast and went to my computer. Yes, I heard the divine correct: "There was a great sale on a travel website that I use regularly for flights to Kona, Hawaii, and one of my favorite hotels!" I also heard, "You need to take Kathy with you if she is guided to go." I had already checked out the seat sale before I called my friend Kathy.

Kathy is an amazing soul full of love and warmth. She answered the phone and I said to her, "Are you ready to go on a spontaneous vacation?" She said, "I don't know. Where and when?" I said, "To Kona, Hawaii, in two days?" She laughed and said, "I can't do that. I have three boys. Who will watch them? What will my husband say?" I asked her to tap into her heart and see what she was guided to do regarding this trip. I wanted her to own her decisions as I did mine. She said she would call me back soon.

Kathy returned my phone call after she did her angel cards and tapped into her own intuitive wisdom and said, "Yes I am coming. I have never booked a trip on such short notice. I am so excited, I feel like a child."

So off Kathy and I went to Kona, Hawaii! While we were in Hawaii, we spent a lot of time in the ocean cleansing our auric fields and chakras, crying, laughing, resting and meditating. I know that Pele and her sister Snow Mountain goddess have activated much dormant energy within my soul and have healed many wounds that I was ready to have healed. I will always be truly grateful for those fun times of being spontaneous, following my divine guidance and knowing that it will all work out in the end. At first, I had to really shut out the naysayers who would make negative comments about me leaving my children with my husband for a week and going to Hawaii. When I looked into those comments, those people were empty inside and really needed to be filled up but couldn't put them first without feeling guilt. We need to remember to fill up our cup first. However that looks for you may be different from it looks for someone else. It is important not to judge others.

I have channeled almost all of my healing meditations with the goddesses while in Kona, Hawaii. I find the support of the ocean, the elementals, and the fiery energy of Pele really support my spiritual needs while I am channeling these ancient words to share with others. I have found that the more I heal myself, the more powerful my meditations and workshops are for others who listen to my meditations and use my healing crystals. I can see that my increased vibration is shifting others who are ready, in a very loving way. As I gain the confidence and strength to step into my true self through healing and receiving activations, I can see dramatic shifting in those souls who are doing my channeled work.

It continues to amaze me at the shifts that I am seeing and hearing in the comments from women and men who have done the work that I have done previously. I feel like I am amplifying the healing words of my meditations and teachings. This information just clicked for me a few months ago. It was my light-bulb moment.

As I allow myself to truly trust in the divine and allow the words to be channeled through me, without letting my left brain get involved in the editing process, I can see how each meditation gets stronger and heals at a deeper vibrational level. I am healing myself first going through all of the steps, and then I am able to share my experiences and act as a clear quartz crystal amplifying the healing for all others wishing to heal and empower their lives with this ancient goddess knowledge.

When I first started taking my natural health practitioner diploma, I knew that I could run energy from a higher power through my hands yet I didn't have any teachings on this type of healing yet. I would tell some people that I could naturally heal their pain and that I had not taken a reiki course or any hands on healing at this point in time. This information would make some clients uncomfortable and they wouldn't return to see me again. So then I decided to take my reiki levels one and two from an amazing reiki master and shaman, Sandy Day, who I had been seeing for a few years. I thought that I would get these tools and add them to my tool kit to make my healing sessions even more unique. Then I could finally tell my clients that I was doing reiki, which would ease their human fears of *magic* healing.

The last meditation that I channeled before finishing this book was with Ixchel, the Mayan moon goddess. In this meditation, she has you open up your eight chakras and connect to the Seven Ancient Wonders of the World, sending healing energy

Velva Dawn Silver-Hughes

to those sacred places on Earth and also to receive an activation to amplify your own natural healing abilities. When I was using Ixchel's meditation for the first time, it was a sunny, quiet day and I was guiding my class through the meditation. When I started to connect their chakras to the energy of these seven ancient wonders, there was a huge gust of wind that felt and sounded as if it blew through the retreat center where I was hosting the event. I smiled to myself and thanked the wind for her assistance in the healing. I asked the students when they came out of the meditation if they heard and felt the wind and they all said, "Yes, that was cool!"

So since I have worked with Ixchel I have been given the tools to work with the elements of the moon, the sun, the wind, the Earth, and the water to use in clearing and healing the chakras. We truly are all in spirit form and can shape shift into any element that we wish or need to be.

I personally have been bringing the energy of the moon, the sun, the sisterhood of the stars and the infinite beings of the universe into my chakras daily with the palms of my hands up to the sky pulling in this natural elemental energy to recharge and cleanse my body.

We need to tap into our personal truth and allow ourselves to activate and fully trust in divine guidance. I know that I will be traveling to more sacred sites to receive all of my activations. I am very excited and grateful for this wisdom and guidance.

Crystal Healing

If you wish to place the green amazonite upon your heart or throat chakra for healing for a few minutes each day, this will enhance your trust within yourself and your life path will become clearer. You will begin to live your life pleasing yourself and not worrying so much about what others think.

The amazonite will activate the spiritual warrior within your soul, allowing you to speak your true feelings from your heart. Speech creates our true reality. The amazonite combines the water element representing our emotions with the air element representing our wisdom, a perfect combination to honor the spiritual warrior within.

Affirmation

"Trust your soul—it knows what to do. Follow your intuition and all things will easily fall into place upon your path. Connect your physical body to the elements of nature. Quiet your negative chatter and avoid naysayers in your life, for you will shine like the wise medicine woman/man that you are."

Dedication

I would like to dedicate this chapter to an amazing reiki master and shaman friend, Sandy Day. She truly represents the energy and qualities of Mother Earth with her infinite unconditional motherly love and wisdom. I often refer to Sandy as my Divine Mother.

Chapter 26

———⚬━♣♠♣━⚬———

Lakshmi
Abundance

Color: Bronze
Crystal: Raw Citrine

Lakshmi is the Hindu goddess of wealth and prosperity, both material and spiritual. She is often depicted as having four arms and four hands, wearing red clothing with golden trim, standing on a lotus flower, and being supported by two elephants. Lakshmi has absolute faith in fertility of whatever it is that you are in need of in your life. The water, lotus flower, and elephant all represent fertility and abundance that are available to you in all of the sources that you need.

Abundance is available to all souls that ask for help. The god/goddess doesn't want anyone to suffer in his or her lifetime. Lakshmi pleads for us all to ask her for abundance in any source that we feel that are deficient. She will show us the way to create more of what we need if we ask. If it is more time that we need in our lives, then she will create the flexibility within our schedules so that we may achieve balance. If it is more financial stability that we are wanting, then she will help open the portal connected to your sacral chakra to allow your true creative passion to flow in whatever expression will create increased finances while enjoying what you are doing. If it is health or

a stronger divine connection that you are in need of,
then Lakshmi will help guide you to those resources;
she can also guide you through meditations to help
cleanse your chakras of old inhibiting self-limiting
belief systems, so that you can see more clearly.
Whatever it is that you are wanting to manifest more
of, please ask me.

When I first starting working with Lakshmi's energy, I was seeing rainbows everywhere I looked, whether I was at home on the ranch, traveling across the United States during the summer, or in Hawaii heading toward the rain forest section. There were beautiful rainbows everywhere. My girls know how much I love to take photos of rainbows so as soon as they see a rainbow starting to emerge they run and find me and say, "Mom, you had better get your camera as there is a rainbow!" It is a fun connection I have with my girls, my little goddesses.

As I was seeing more and more rainbows, Lakshmi was telling me to stand with my feet firmly in the ground and look at the all seven rays of the rainbow—ROYGBIV (red, orange, yellow, green, blue, indigo, and violet) like the colors of my chakras—and to ask the rainbow for healing of my chakras by taking in several deep breaths and feeling and visualizing this rainbow energy coming into my heart chakra and then transmuting each color of the rainbow to match each color of my chakra. I was amazed at how I could feel the light and loving energy of the rainbow transmute and flow through all of the cells of my body. I started to teach my daughters how to use the rainbow energy to cleanse and tone their chakras when they see a rainbow.

Lakshmi has also given me the words to a guided meditation using rainbow energy to cleanse and tone your chakras while using programmed clear quartz crystals on your chakras.

Lakshmi said that we have forgotten how to use the rainbow energy for healing purposes within our physical bodies. Many of us enjoy the beauty of the colors of the rainbow but we can now amplify the healing essence of these magnificent arches in the sky after a rainfall or just because!

We need to remember that it never hurts to ask for abundance and that we need not feel greedy because we are asking for more. If we are truly following our life path with passion and awareness, we will receive abundance from the divine in all ways in our life. When we are in the flow of the divine, we are like a rainbow's energy: full of passion and beauty ready to receive the gifts that are bestowed upon us with gratefulness and peace!

As I am typing this chapter I, see that it is 3:33 p.m., which is an affirmation from Lakshmi that divine beings and ascended masters and goddesses surround me. I urge you to look at your surroundings for messages from the goddesses and divine. You are supported on all realms.

Crystal Healing

You may wish to place a raw citrine crystal in the far left-hand corner of your front entrance as it signals to the universe that you are wishing and willing to receive abundance. You may also wish to place a citrine crystal on your sacral or solar plexus chakra to create harmony with the divine will. The first step in creating a manifestation is to write out what your intentions are by creating an energetic blueprint of what it is that you wish to create. The next step is to start the process of this blueprint by speaking and thinking the words that you wish to manifest as your end goal. It is true what you think about you bring about, so ask Lakshmi to help you create a set of affirmations that have a very high vibration and will help physically co-create your manifestation. Using the citrine crystal on either chakra will open up these centers and get your creative thoughts going.

Affirmation

"I deserve abundance in all areas of my life. I am worthy of abundance in health, wealth, friendships, love, laughter, joy, harmony, spiritual connection and all else that I desire. I am open to receiving and grateful for all abundance."

Dedication

I would like to dedicate this chapter to my friend Kellie Cartwright. May you always think abundance and give love.

This is a photo of a rainbow on our ranch that
I took with my camera.

Chapter 27

Maeve

Moon Cycles

Color: Lime Green
Crystal: Gray & White Moonstone

Maeve is a legendary Celtic goddess who is celebrated and honored for her feminine energy. She is known to help women ease the pain of labor when giving birth to a child. She can help alleviate menstrual pain and aid in regulating your menstrual cycles, flow and hormones. Women who are entering menopause may wish to consult with Maeve for assistance. She is strongly connected to the cycles of the universe, the moon and the stars.

> *Please call on me if you are needing to regulate any hormonal issues within your body. You may wish to write me a letter pertaining to your health concerns relating to your menses, labor, or menopause. I am very knowledgeable in the female reproductive system and aligning your feminine energy with the moons, the stars and the universal life force. Once you surrender your female needs to me, I can then assist you with guidance to connect you with the feminine energies of the universe. I have the ancient tools to help you. Please ask for my assistance and I will be there.*

If you are in need of assistance with an irregular menstrual cycle and you have already visited your family physician you may wish to write a letter to Maeve asking her for divine intervention and please let go of all thoughts on how this might happen. Get a calendar that you will use to mark down the beginning date of your menstrual flow and the end date. Keep track for a few months and begin to look how the beginning of your menstrual flow corresponds to the full moon, meaning it is close to the first day of the full moon. Maeve strongly suggests that you connect with your uterus, ovaries and hormones and ask them if they are willing to work with the energy of the moon and the stars. If you hear or feel that the answer is yes, then you are ready for the next step. If you hear or feel the answer is no, then you must ask why your body isn't ready to work with these energies.

It could be a past life wound that perhaps your body doesn't want to give up or doesn't want to change. If this is so, then please ask your higher self to let go of these old wounds and, while breathing deeply, ask Artemis to dissolve any energetic webbing that might still be attached to your female reproductive organs. Then ask Mother Mary to use her gentle, wise hands to send healing to these organs, to heal all wounds. You may feel some tingling and your lower abdomen may truly feel lighter. This would be a good exercise for every woman to do before you ask for the realignment ceremony from Maeve.

New Moon

Watch the calendar for the next new moon and write a letter to Maeve, Sister Luna, to the sisterhood of the stars and the universe to give permission to allow the initiation ceremony of the realignment of your reproductive organs and female energy with the feminine sisterhood of the universe. The new moon is a symbol of new beginnings. In this letter, you may wish to specifically outline what it is that you need healing within your female organs. This could a regular, normal-flowing menstrual cycle, fertility to have a baby, healing of a sexually transmitted disease, help with menopause night sweats, premenstrual syndrome pain and mood swings. You may wish to ask that the first day of your menstrual flow will start on the first day of the full moon. Whatever it is, please outline it specifically and at the end of the letter please write a sentence of gratitude to all involved.

On the night of the new moon, please take a gray moonstone crystal, fold your letter in three, and hold the letter to your heart, thanking Maeve for the divine assistance with your feminine energy. Place the letter outside, if weather is permitting, where the moon's rays can shine on the letter. Place the gray moonstone on top of the letter.

This crystal represents the new moon and will be one of your healing symbols from this night forward by connecting your feminine energy with the sisterhood of the universe to amplify the wishes in your letter.

If you are not able to put the letter and the crystal outside due to bad weather, then please place the letter in a window that will see the moon's rays on the evening of the new moon.

You may wish to make a healing elixir to help you through this realignment process. To do this you must use a very natural source of water and no chlorine in the water. Buy natural spring water if you have to and ask for guidance from Maeve while you are shopping for it. Please use a large glass pitcher to fill with your natural spring water. Then place the gray moonstone in the pitcher full of water and put it outside the night before the actual new moon is scheduled. Ask Maeve, Sister Luna, and the sisterhood of the stars, and the universe to bless this water and give them permission to send their healing wisdom essence through the molecules of the water and the gray moonstone crystal. Once again, if it is cold outside don't leave the water outside all night. A few hours will be fine. Also remember to cover the top of the water pitcher with saran wrap so that it remains clean from any foreign objects or a pet that might be thirsty.

Start a journal specifically for this healing process. After the new moon, take a minute first thing in the morning to talk with your female organs and feminine energy and see what messages she has for you. You may also wish to sense how your female organs feel. Your uterus may feel lighter and smaller. Note that you also may go through a process of cleansing and you may start your menses earlier than planned. Your flow may be heavier at first to clear all negative and lower energies that may be stored in the sacral and root chakras.

The next night following the new moon please, place the gray moonstone crystal under your pillow to remain there until the night before the next full moon. You may also wish to place the green moonstone on your sacral or root chakra during meditation for a few minutes daily to help ease any discomfort you may have. You can also carry the crystal in your left pocket to receive this healing energy.

Full Moon

The night before the full moon, you may wish to have a white moonstone crystal ready for your use. We will be using the white moonstone crystal as it is associated with releasing and has a strong connection to the full moon. You may wish to hold the crystal in your left hand, thanking it for extending its healing vibrations to you. As always, before you use a crystal, make sure to cleanse it either by smudging with sage, putting it in a bowl of water with a pinch of Dead Sea salt, placing it in a singing bowl and playing it, or in a natural stream of water to clear all negative or lower energies from its auric field.

You may also wish to make a full moon healing elixir with your white moonstone crystal. Make it the same way as you prepared to make the new moon elixir with the gray moonstone, but put the pitcher of water with the white moonstone in it out the night before the full moon is scheduled. Then once again ask Maeve, Sister Luna, the Sisterhood of the Stars, and the Universe to bless and send their healing essence through the molecules of the water with the rays of the full moon. If possible, please leave this full moon pitcher outside for four nights. If the weather doesn't permit, then you can put it in a window for four nights. You can pour the water into a large blue bottle to keep for use until the next new moon.

I will sometimes put two to four ounces of moon elixir in a crystal glass and will add some of my spring water to sip throughout the day, or you can drink it as a shot of pure moon elixir first thing in the morning.

Make sure that you take the crystal out of the water after the four days, as you will need to place the white moonstone under your pillow until the night before the next scheduled new moon.

So, as you can see, the cycles that we will be adjusting with our female energies do in fact honor the cycles of the moon, stars and universe. We are connecting to the ancient wisdom of feminine hood that we knew years ago. We have moved away from connecting with these energies due to artificial hormones and spiritual disconnects. Our bodies are made of water and greatly crave the healing water infused with the natural energies of the goddesses, crystals, the moon, the stars and the universe.

Crystal Healing

Use the gray and white moonstone as outlined above for the full moon and the new moon.

Affirmation

"May your feminine and masculine energies be in harmony within your physical body, while deeply rooted into Mother Earth and divinely connected to the wisdom of the moon, the stars and the universe."

Dedication

I would like to dedicate this chapter to my sister moon goddess Chris DeRoo.

My sister the full moon

Chapter 28

―――o·ᙇᙇo――――

Nemetona

Insight

Color: Peacock Blue
Crystal: Azurite

Nemetona is the goddess who will help you connect with the divine so that you may gain insight into your life. She is a Celtic goddess whose name represents "sacred land." She watches over and protects sacred sites around the planet. Nemetona is very connected to nature, the elements and the divine. She will also help you create a divine altar to represent your dreams and goals.

Please ask me to assist you in creating a sacred space to represent the energy of where you would like your soul to be. I will help you attain the clarity and time to set these goals and a space. I would also love to help you with any insights that may make your steps along your life path easier and more harmonious. I can give you these insights in dreams and I will help you interpret them if you need. I am very connected with nature so when you are outdoors please call upon me for any divine needs you have or wish to gain clarity on, or ask for help with assistance in creating a sacred space or altar for yourself.

One night while I was sleeping I had the craziest dream. I was at my parents' home and we were all outside the house and there was an airplane flying over us and we had received news that it was going to crash. All of us were outside the house, except for our three girls who were playing inside my parents' house. I had a really strong feeling that I needed to run and get them out of the house. My mom and dad said, "Don't worry. The plane won't crash on the house; they will be safer inside." The feeling kept growing stronger within my stomach and I started running until I reached the house. I went inside and told the girls to come with me. We ran out to where everyone was standing. Soon, I could see that the airplane was in fact diving toward my parents' home. The airplane did crash into their house and blew up with a huge explosion. I looked at everyone and said, "See, I knew that was going to happen," and I was go glad that I had followed my intuitive feelings.

I awoke that morning and thought, *Okay, what was that dream about? Should I be flying on an airplane with caution?* I tapped into the dream, communicating with Nemetona by asking her if I should be careful when flying. She said not to worry. The dream wasn't about flying but the message would be revealed soon.

A few weeks later, Stephen and I had a weekend planned to go to my cousin's wedding in Medicine Hat, Alberta. We had made arrangements to stay in the same hotel as my aunt Germaine and uncle Dick. Our girls were going to stay with Stephen's dad Jim for a couple of nights.

We left early that morning, as it was about a four-hour drive to get to the wedding. It was a beautiful June morning. The sun was shining and it was a warm day. We had all gathered at my parents' travel trailer as they were staying at a campground in town for the wedding. We were visiting and catching up with family about each other's lives. My uncle Dick was always entertaining everyone with his dry sense of humor and smile. We all attended my cousin's beautiful wedding ceremony in the afternoon and then went out for a nice supper before the dance started later on that evening. My uncle Dick decided that he would like to pay for all of our meals for supper that evening. He was joking with the waitress and all of us around him with his quick wit. I remember him saying to the waitress, "I am a wise one," and he was laughing to himself. I was thinking, *Yes you really are a wise one with knowledge from many past lives.* He was always observing everyone, a man of few words, but he never missed a thing!

After a nice supper, we all drove to the hall where the wedding dance was being held. We all went inside and had photos taken of each couple. I thought that this was a great idea, as most couples don't have photos of themselves at nice occasions like weddings when we are all dressed up.

We went to sit down and get ready for the dance to start when my mom came rushing up to my aunt Germaine, Stephen and me and told us that uncle Dick was outside and wasn't feeling very well and that we should all come out to check on him.

When we got outside, my dad was standing by my aunt and uncle's van and Uncle Dick was gray in color. He told my aunt Germaine to get in the van and drive him back to the hotel. I could see that he was very ill and had a very bad feeling about the whole situation.

My aunt drove off in the van to the hotel. I asked my dad if Uncle Dick had said anything about how he was feeling. He said he was feeling nauseous in the hall so he decided to come outside for some fresh air, and that he accompanied him to make sure that he was okay. Then Uncle Dick told Dad that he thought his blood sugars were elevated as he had diabetes, and he was going to lie down in the van for a bit. This is the point where I came out and saw my uncle.

My parents, Stephen and I were standing outside the hall and discussing what we thought we should do, if anything. I said to everyone, "I think that Uncle Dick is having a heart attack and that we should go back to the hotel and make sure he goes to the hospital." My dad is very conservative and private and told me that we should not disturb them if they wanted to be left alone. Then the dream that I had a couple of weeks ago about the airplane crashing into my parents' house started to circulate through my mind. I kept getting a very strong feeling that we needed to go check on my aunt and uncle immediately and that I needed to not listen to my dad at this time. So Stephen and I got in our vehicle and my parents decided to come with us. My mom agreed with me that she thought he was having a heart attack, as she has a nursing background.

When we arrived at the hotel, my aunt's van was parked next to the lobby of the hotel. I could see my uncle Dick lying on the floor in the middle of the van trying to sit up to get out of the van. I could see that he was in a lot of pain and fighting for his life. His face was completely gray and he was vomiting.

We all walked up to their van, wanting to help them, to call an ambulance. My uncle Dick got very angry and told us to go away from the van. He then made my aunt Germaine move the van farther away from the lobby into an empty space in the parking lot of the hotel. I kept hearing Nemetona saying, "This event right now relates to your dream. Follow your intuition and call for help. Your uncle is dying." I kept saying to my dad, "We need to call for an ambulance. He is dying!" Everyone was running their diagnosis through the group, wondering if it was food poisoning or diabetes out of control. Then finally my dad agreed that he was going to call an ambulance.

As he was about to call 911, we could see that an ambulance was heading toward the parking lot of our hotel. My uncle had finally allowed my aunt to call for help. My dad flagged the ambulance driver over to their van. Then we all went over to be with my aunt, as I knew she was very shocked and stressed. My uncle Dick was being loaded onto the stretcher and into the back of the ambulance when we saw him. He was answering some questions that the paramedics were asking him. The ambulance took him to the local hospital, which was only a few minutes away. We drove to meet up with them.

As my mom and I walked down the hospital corridor to find the emergency waiting room where my aunt was, we saw the emergency room doctor walking toward the waiting room. I knew that there was something very wrong with my uncle Dick.

The doctor told us that my uncle Dick had suffered a massive heart attack and had passed away en route to the hospital. He asked my aunt to come and say good-bye to my uncle and that we should go to be with her. I remember standing at the foot of his bed and thinking that this can't be happening now! I was angry that this had happened again, another death in our family so soon after the others, *and why at a wedding?*

We were all in shock trying to figure out what to do next. I had contacted a funeral home to come and get my uncle's body the next day and take him to a funeral home near where they lived. My parents had their travel trailer and it was late at night by this time. It was 11:00 p.m. and dark, so they didn't want to drive their fifth wheel home in the dark. I volunteered to drive my aunt home that night, with Stephen following us in our vehicle. I went back to the hotel and told the front desk staff that my uncle Dick had passed away and that we needed to check out immediately. We gathered up our suitcases and started the four-hour drive home.

As I was driving along the highway, I could hear my uncle Dick talking to me already in spirit form. He was confused about what had just happened. He wanted me to tell my aunt Germaine that I could talk to him, and that I should tell her this at this moment. He was persistent so after a bit I did tell my aunt that I could talk to angels and the deceased if she ever felt inclined to do so. I told my uncle Dick that I would talk to him later as I needed to absorb what had just happened.

It was a very long drive home that night, but I was grateful to be of service to both my aunt and uncle. I had moved to the city to work for both of them the summer after I graduated from high school. As I mentioned previously, my uncle Dick was a quiet, wise man who observed everything that went on, even though he didn't speak about it. I felt an instant connection with him and understood who he truly was.

I knew that we had planned to attend my cousin's wedding together for that very reason that he wanted me to be there to shine the light for him when he passed. I felt very honored and humbled by this experience.

As we were sitting at his funeral service a few days later, I heard Nemetona talking to me again, telling me that I was strong enough to handle these situations. That is why I was there when this occurred and that I needed to pay special attention to my dreams as they did foretell the future.

My parents, Stephen, and I, were feeling terribly guilty for months after my uncle's death that we didn't call the ambulance sooner and that he might still be alive. I was having nightmares about the event. Then someone told me that everything happens for a reason and that my uncle Dick died on the night of a full moon, when the veil is very thin, which made it easy for him to get to the light. She told me that he had planned this exit and was ready to go and that it had all played out the way he wanted it to. This advice helped me feel at peace with it all.

I urge you to ask Nemetona for insight into your life and to help you create your own sacred space to connect with the divine. She assisted me through this difficult period in my life by urging me to trust my intuition, so that I was able to be with my aunt Germaine that day that Uncle Dick passed away. I listened to her when she told me to go to the hotel to check on them, and then to drive immediately to the hospital to be with my aunt when the doctor walked in to tell her that her husband had passed away. To be there to help assist my uncle Dick to the light was a blessing to me!

Crystal Healing

Please place the blue azurite crystal on your third eye, closing both of your physical eyes, which allows your inner site to adjust and become focused. Please turn your energy within and invoke the essence of the azurite to help you see what it is that you are ready to see. This crystal will also lend us the inner sight to perceive where our motives are based. This is a very powerful crystal for awakening your clairvoyance.

Affirmation

"I am divinely connected to my intuition, honoring and trusting all that it is trying to tell me. I am a divine being who is clairvoyant, clairaudient, clairsentient, and claircognizant."

Dedication

I would like to dedicate this chapter to Germaine Ellis.

Chapter 29

Rhiannon

Inner Sorceress

Color: Luminescent White
Crystal: Selenite

Rhiannon is the goddess who can create alchemy in ways that are unheard of. She has the ability to change the weather, create the wind to blow, ask the sun to shine, and create the land that she needs. Rhiannon rides upon a white horse, even a unicorn in some lifetimes.

> *She has the ability to create absolute magic with her healing abilities using crystals, divine energy from Mother Earth, and Father Sky, and all of the natural elements. She creates what she needs in her life at the time. She can foresee if she needs to alter the future. She can communicate with all life in many different ways. She is a strong and independent goddess who wants to teach her ways in this lifetime, carrying the vibrations of love and light. She feels the need to bring forward this positive magical energy into the world today. Mother Earth needs our help to keep her planet alive and sustainable. Rhiannon is asking all light workers who are interested in crystals and healing to please put the call out to her and she will teach you how to help with this huge mission.*

She has asked me to be a primary spiritual teacher for this task and I have gratefully accepted her invitation. I am teaching other light workers how to use this energy and will be writing books specifically with information from her.

She knows that in past lives using crystals and magic has gotten a bad rap, and that those words scare off a lot of people and have created a lot of fear. I am here to teach her ways from the ancient times in our modern times but to bring them forward with love and light and the purest intentions.

Rhiannon is also saying that she will help plants, herbs and flowers grow along with the fairies but we need to ask her to help us.

She led a life of divine magic, which made her life a lot easier. She would see some of the *common* people have rough times in their lives because no one had shown them how to access the divine energy to create a harmonious and easy life. Rhiannon felt that her time was way too short to teach those that she needed to teach so she is very excited to be sharing her wisdom by channeling for this book.

Rhiannon would jump on her white horse and fly through the green fields with her golden hair flowing in the wind. She had total trust in her friend, her white horse. She knew that he would carry her wherever she needed to go. Rhiannon too could communicate with animals by using her intuition and feeling the energy with her hands. She would use crystals to heal herself and those around her, even her animals. She would cleanse her crystals in the riverbed streams that flowed along with nature. She would often place her crystals in the river, in a stone circle that she had built by placing river stones in a circle and then building up the layers of the circle. She would place her crystals in this cleansing circle the night before the full moon each month to clear them of all negative and lower energies. Next, she would place the crystals in the sunset to amplify their energies and re-energize the matrix of the crystals. She knew exactly what to do with each crystal. She could feel the vibration of each one and knew what healing properties each crystal had for thousands of ailments.

She would like us to remember that we once used high vibrating raw crystals to treat our health issues, to clear our homes, our chakras, our animals, plants, and families. She said that these crystals would be the key to aid in prevention of disease in our physical body by keeping our auras clean and large. Crystals are easy to use. Just respect them and they will respect you. They are living beings also.

> *The crystals can be combined with the elements of nature to amplify their abilities: the moon, the sun, the water, the wind, and the Earth. All of the elements can be used to clear the crystals.*

When buying crystals, hold them and feel their energy before paying for them; it is best if you can see them in person when buying crystals and see what type of energy is in the store that is selling the crystals. If the owner and staff of the metaphysical stores aren't practicing clearing their own energy fields and aren't passionate about selling crystals, then the energy in the crystals won't be as high as other stores with balanced and staff. If the crystals are happy then buy them. They will have amazing benefits for you.

Spending time outdoors with animals is also a good way to create magical energy to help in clearing, manifesting, or healing energies.

Rhiannon's wish for all of the goddesses out there is to find some crystals that are calling to you. Carry them and get to know them and what they can do for you. Learn to use them on your children. Get to know the different healing abilities for each crystal. Buy a crystal book that has the meanings and healing modalities in it. You will find that your children will love to use the crystals; they are healthy and have no negative side effects as long as they are used properly and with respect. So the next time your child has a headache, call upon Rhiannon and ask her what crystal you should give to your child and then ask her to guide you as you clear the energy around your child so that you can try to do the healing naturally. She isn't saying not to contact your doctor if need be, but if it is something simple try to fix it using your intuition, the goddesses, and some crystals.

My oldest daughter Kayla had a headache and I thought, *Okay, I am going to fix this naturally.* So I used my hand to feel the energy around her head, and sure enough there was a cord attached to the right side of the base of her skull. I asked Archangel Michael and Artemis to help me cut this cord and I also asked Archangel Raphael and Jesus to send light and love to where the cord was attached to her and to the other person. Then I had her place an amethyst crystal on her third eye until the headache dissipated. Sure enough, within one hour the pain went away and we did it naturally!

So trust your intuition, feel your way through life and go with your gut when you feel you should. Be strong enough to trust your inner self and say "no" when you need to or try something different if you feel the need to.

Invoke Rhiannon the sorceress and find the magic goddess within yourself to heal any aspect of your life that needs to be healed.

I have recorded a channeled meditation from Rhiannon that ignites the union of the feminine and masculine energies within your physical body and will help bring forth your Sanskrit name from a past life and healing techniques to use in this lifetime.

Crystal Healing

Please place the white selenite crystal at your crown chakra to help open the doorway to your higher self. The opening of this chakra will allow the energy of the divine to flow through your physical body to heal all that needs to be healed.

Affirmation

"I am a divine being of natural magic and can heal all of my body's ailments that need healing, using my recipes from long ago."

Dedication

I would like to dedicate this chapter to our horse Pegasus; she is the horse on the cover of my Rhiannon meditation.

Pegasus (mother to Luna), a magical mare

Chapter 30

―⊶∂₰ℬ₰∞―

Sekhmet

Feminine Strength & Grace

Color: Navy Blue
Crystal: Sodalite

Sekhmet is often depicted as having a lion's head and a woman's body. She is an Egyptian sun goddess. She has the strength of a lioness yet the gentle balance of the feline feminine spirit. She walks like a cat, very strong and wise, and she portrays grace and dignity.

Now is the time, here on Earth, that we need to align ourselves with our true spiritual self. We need to walk our talk, truly from the very depth of our soul. We need to take time each day to connect with our higher self and ask for the courage to take the next step on our spiritual path, to align ourselves with the divine strength until we can truly feel it within.

Sekhmet asks that each morning we take a few minutes to go outdoors to give gratitude to the sun for her beautiful rays of love and light. As you are sitting outside absorbing her healing rays, ask that your purest intentions be spread out into the universe by seeing your healing thoughts and kind prayers travel through the sun's rays up into the very center vortex of the sun, then amplified and spread out into the universe to magnify your deepest loving intentions for yourself and for the world. Remember to include a loving message for yourself first, the world, and then the universe. It is not selfish to care for your wishes first. We all need love and the sun goddess wishes to help magnify and transmute your loving thoughts to others. She asks that you remember her, and that she is willing to help but needs your permission and thoughts first.

Allow your loving thoughts and prayers to build energy within your heart center as you sit quietly and bring forth these loving intentions. Please feel your heart center expanding and yearning for healing, loving messages to enter this space. When you are guided to, move those thoughts up to your throat chakra, then your third-eye chakra, and finally up and out of your crown chakra. Send these beams of love to sister Sun. You may feel the healing radiating up and out, being magnified by the heat of yellow rays. Remember to put on sunscreen if the sun is intense to protect your skin and envision a rainbow iridescent pyramid surrounding your body to reflect any intense sunrays.

I seem to learn my life lessons at a very strong and rapid pace and need to move forward in my spiritual evolution at an accelerated rate compared to others. As I reflect upon these lessons, I am proud and grateful how easily I can move through these energy steps aided by the wisdom and healing techniques from the goddesses.

Recently I traveled to Hawaii to take a course and to be part of a group facilitation that I thought would fulfill a lifelong dream for me.

As soon as I agreed to this task, I didn't feel right about the energy surrounding the event that I was asked to assist with. My gut kept telling me to cancel my flight and stay home, but my head kept telling me to go. I decided that there was a reason that I was going on this journey even though my intuition kept telling me that it might not turn out the way that I had envisioned it. This is an important thing to remember when visualizing your goals. Do not put limits or close doors to any opportunities by visualizing exact happenings of an event. Allow the divine to give you what you deserve and you probably won't be able to visualize something that grand for yourself. So please don't put barriers up regarding goals that you wishing to fulfill.

So off I went to Hawaii, a magical healing place for me, with my good friend Kathy. As soon as we were about to land, I could feel my energy connect with Pele, the goddess of the volcanoes in Hawaii. She warned me that something might not go as I had planned on this trip.

As soon as we arrived at our hotel where the event was being held, the obstacles were flying like red flags for me to see.

My stomach was unsettled and I was feeling that there was something very different about to happen this weekend.

I felt invisible to the other staff members during this time. I was feeling like I was from another planet, which I am. The communication was completely broken down. The lady who had asked me to help with the event was ill, so I programmed a crystal healing kit for her to ease her pain and help facilitate healing if she so desired.

I had also programmed a healing kit for the facilitator, as a gift from my heart to her, thanking her for sharing her wealth of intuitive wisdom to help me along my spiritual path.

The next morning, I sat in the restaurant, having breakfast with Kathy. All of the other staff members walked by me without any acknowledgment. I observed as they gathered and laughed with each other. My friend Kathy was angry that they had not spoken to me nor had they tried to include me in their gathering. I too was feeling hurt and angry but wasn't sure yet how to deal with the situation.

My mind was racing in circles. My ego was jumping in, telling me, "I told you so." So I sat quietly overlooking the ocean and began asking the goddesses and the divine what next step I should take.

As I walked out of the restaurant, I was guided to step into my power. I ignited my goddess flame with Isis. Immediately, I could feel that my power center had expanded and I felt ready to deal with anything that came my way. I walked over to the building where the course was going to be held. I prayed for strength from Sekhmet, as I knew the staff was meeting in this building before the day got under way. I knocked on the door and asked if they needed any help. "Yes," was the answer. "Please come in and here is the schedule for the day."

Wow, I thought, *I must have been making up all of those negative feelings that I had been feeling previously.* I jumped in and helped out in any way that I could for the day, observing how things really were on the *other* side—I had always been an attendee for many years previous.

As the day went by I sat there with a knowing that this wasn't where I was supposed to be. Being staff, I knew that I was to be teaching and empowering other people by being a leader. I wanted to give back to my *spiritual guru* who had enlightened my life by words, books, and meditations.

The next morning, the phone rang at 6:30 a.m. with the woman who had asked me to help at the event in tears, saying that I needed to come and talk with her in person, that there had been a terrible miscommunication. As you can imagine, I was in shock and wondered what was happening to this amazing weekend that I had always wanted to experience.

As I walked over to the meeting room to speak with this woman, I passed another staff member in the hallway. Being intuitive, I could feel the pain in her heart because she knew what I was about to experience.

As I moved one foot in front of the other, I knew I was surrounded by Sekhmet's strong gracious energy. She was helping me hold my head up high as I intuitively knew something about this conversation was going to hurt. As I walked into the room, this wonderful soul was crying, saying that she didn't know why the facilitator was so upset about me helping with this event. I could see the pain in her husband's eyes and her daughter's eyes. The friendship between the facilitator and her event coordinator was rocky and now damaged with words of distrust and dishonor. An anger arose from within me, and I said to this woman, "Why would your friend treat you this way when you are ill? How could she be like this?"

The tears started to gently roll down my face, with anger and hurt swelling within my solar plexus and heart. I was thinking, *How can this dream of helping my* spiritual guru *end like this? How can someone who is so aligned with her higher self treat others like this? What is happening to my whole world? I never saw this coming . . . or did I?*

I gave this loving woman a hug, sending her love from my heart to hers, albeit still stunned by what had just happened over the last thirty minutes. I told her that in no circumstances was it okay for anyone to treat her like this, especially when she was ill.

I walked back to my room to tell my friend Kathy what had happened. We both cried, hurt and in shock as to why this had happened the way it did.

I could feel this inner strength guiding me and encouraging me to act with the highest dignity and courage. I then phoned a mutual friend of all of ours and told her what had happened. She told me that it had nothing to do with me personally, but that I was part of the soul group that needed to be involved with the process. I agreed with her and decided to take the high road, pack up my things, and head to my favorite beach to process the events of the last few days.

I was feeling empathy for my friend Kathy, who had to finish off her course from the facilitator who had just asked me to pack up and not finish staffing the event. I knew that it would be hard for Kathy to sit and listen to the facilitator speak those words, knowing what had just happened behind the scenes.

When I drove down the highway for forty-five minutes to get to the beach where we were staying for the next two nights, I felt as though I was floating, knowing that I wasn't in my body. I sat on the beach crying, feeling thoughts of becoming a victim out there, and lying in the fetal position in my bed for the next month. I felt shame. I was hurt, bitter and did not want to trust the divine.

As I was lying there hearing the ocean continually flowing, I heard that this lesson was a gift to me. I tend to have the very strong personality of an Aries, and a number one in numerology, so I needed a strong spiritual leader to put me back on my own life path immediately. I heard that this is no time for me to be a victim; I am a role model for so many and being a victim is so past life for me.

I connected with the spiritual guru's higher self and told her how I felt, telling her that I couldn't forgive her at this point but I would work on it.

I then drove back to get my friend Kathy from her course, from the hotel that I had left early in the morning with my sunglasses on, not wanting anyone to see me, hiding in shame. My phone rang as I as sat waiting for her to come out of the building. It was our mutual friend Christina asking how I was doing. She told me that our mutual friend, the lady who had asked me to help at the event, had wanted her to check on me and see how I was doing. She told Christina that I had handled the whole ordeal with grace and that she was so impressed. Christina agreed with her, saying, "What else would you expect from her?"

At this moment I felt a very strong sense of healing and pride; as I looked back upon these two days, I felt proud of how I handled my emotions and thoughts, knowing that I rose above the drama and that I do live my life aligned with my spirituality. I walk my talk, and that it doesn't matter what anyone else does in this world. All that matters is that I honor myself and I did that simple yet powerful act. I received one of the greatest lessons in this lifetime, having my *spiritual guru* give me this gift of knocking down all of the pedestals that I had ever built under others that I chose to view as a more enlightened being than I. The lesson that I received from Sekhmet, and this trip, is that all of the wisdom that you need is within your very soul. Trust in yourself, and just because someone else has channeled wisdom doesn't mean that she or he isn't human; these people are just like you and I: *human.* They too have lessons to learn. I still feel that the golden rule (Do unto others as you would have them do unto you.) is something that we all need to strive for while being human. You are a perfect fragment of God and always look for the gifts in the situation, forgive and move onto your next step. You are a divine being, connected and loving.

Crystal Healing

You may wish to place the sodalite crystal on your throat chakra to begin your spiritual journey. You may wish to look at where you have been and how you have honored yourself during those times, to see if there is any healing that needs to be done on your throat chakra. Honor yourself as the temple that you have created. Explore and create what it is that you are wishing to do at this moment in time.

Affirmation

"I am my own spiritual guru. I am whole, complete, and filled with infinite wisdom to answer any questions I might have. I am always connected to the divine and can receive extra strength when I need it. I walk with grace and a smile upon my beautiful face."

Dedication

I would like to dedicate this chapter to Karen Davidson, a wonderful, intuitive woman.

The sun setting in Hawaii!

Chapter 31

Sige

Self-Reflection

Color: Periwinkle
Crystal: Sugilite

Sige is the Gnostic goddess of silence from which all creation originates. She is the goddess that reminds us that we need to take some quiet time each day to connect with our true self. Our wisdom is created from being quiet and meditating. Sige is the goddess who will help you quiet your mind and go deep within.

One of the most important things that we can do while we are in physical form on Earth is to be still in our minds, for even a few minutes every day, to connect with the divine source. It is important that we push away our negative self-chatter and business to schedule in time for connection directly to the source.

Each morning, take a few minutes before you start your day to quiet your mind in your sacred space and listen to what your higher self and all divine beings wish to tell you. You can ask for guidance in a neutral position from the source, knowing that your answers will be of the utmost highest vibration for you. You may not always like the guidance that you get, as sometimes you will be pushed to step out of your comfort zone and reach new heights so that you can fully embrace the life path that you are meant to follow on this Earth. Taking these few minutes each morning will help set the tone and vibration for your entire day. You will be able to make decisions with confidence and clarity, and your physical body will get the harmonious attention that it needs to remain healthy.

You may also wish to take a few minutes each night before going to sleep to meditate and give thanks for all of the blessings that you may have received during the day. You may also wish to state an intention before going to sleep. You may wish to have a soul visitation from a deceased loved one, or you may wish to astral travel to learn more about your past lives. This will enable you to bring forth new activations for your soul. Whatever your intention might be, send it out to the universe with love.

It is very important for your mental, spiritual, physical, and energetic health that you take some quiet time daily to connect with your divine source whatever that may look like for you. Please ask Sige to help you carve out this time during your day and night. She will be glad to assist you.

As I am channeling this final chapter in this book, I am in divine awe of that fact that the last chapter is with Sige and it is about the importance of self-reflection and meditation. What a perfect ending to the wisdom of the goddesses to share with everyone.

The birth of the wisdom of this book was born from meditating and asking deep within my soul what it is exactly that I am going to do next on my life path. When I heard the guidance that I was going to write many books, produce my own oracle cards, make healing elixirs, teach empowerment workshops, create crystal healing kits, do a series of channeled healing meditations with the goddesses, receive many activations from past lifetimes, and have a family, I started to go into panic mode. I started channeling this book over three years ago, and slowly did a bit at a time. Then I very strongly received the guidance that I had to complete the rough draft of this book by December 31, 2010, as I was going to receive another activation and wouldn't be able to channel the wisdom from the goddesses at the vibration that I needed to share the information in this first book.

When I looked at the outline of the book, I had thirty-one chapters, and in my mind I had written most of them, but my laptop showed a different story. I still needed to finish seventeen chapters out of the thirty-one in thirty-one days, which included a week in Las Vegas celebrating my friend Michelle's fortieth birthday and flying to Mesa, Arizona, to spend nine days with my parents for the Christmas holidays—all while the girls were out of school during Christmas!

As you can imagine, I allowed my physical body to feel the stress at first as I was thinking, *How will this be humanly possible to finish that many chapters in that short amount of time?*

My friend Fawna said, "If anyone can bend time, it's you!" I prayed for assistance in helping me be present during these two vacations for myself and to enjoy the time with my family. I asked that I may feel peace in my physical body and that I be an efficient channel for the goddess wisdom to flow through me. My husband was very supportive in taking the girls while I sat in my office full of crystals and divine goddess energy, typing the words of wisdom to finish this book.

Sige helped me with meditating daily, even hourly or by the minute, to be able to slow down my mind chatter and know that I could complete this task with grace and ease. At the beginning of writing this book, I had a lot of negative voices in my head telling me that no one would read my book and that people would think that I was crazy to channel this book from the goddesses. It has taken a continual daily practice of connection with the divine source and the goddesses to move forth on my path with being an author. I have many good friends who have believed in this book and me and have helped me see it to completion. I thank Chris Marmes from deep within my soul for helping me be accountable to my spirit guides and the goddesses to finish this book.

As I reflect upon the chapters in this book, I can see the self-growth that I have gone through in my physical and spiritual life to further my ascension process. If you are willing to quiet your mind, trust your intuition, cleanse your auric field, leap into action that will propel your self-growth, love yourself, forgive your past wounds, and join with the divine hands of the goddesses and the divine source, you *will* feel a sense of peace and accomplishment in your soul from all of the steps that you have taken to reach the top of your world.

Sige has helped me through these last few years of completing this book and has helped me work through many transformations of my soul! I know that she will be there for the shifts that will occur in my future. Trust in your own ascension process, that you are a divine being of love, and embrace your power with love and light!

Crystal Healing

You may wish to place the purple sugilite crystal above your head on the top of your crown chakra. This crystal will stimulate your crown chakra, encouraging vivid dreams, stimulating psychic and mental abilities, and helping you remember your true divine purpose. You may wish to use this crystal to enhance your daydreams and night dreams and then journal your dreams so that you may reveal insights about yourself in these dreams. The sugilite will allow you to trust in your divine path and gain full clarity on your heart's dreams.

Affirmation

"Blessings to you all. May you each receive the healings and wisdom that you need. May you learn to trust and enjoy the wisdom of the goddesses. May you take the quality time to use self-reflection as a mirror to show you the growth that you have made in your life."

Dedication

I would like to dedicate this chapter to all of the thirty-three goddesses who helped me compile this book of wisdom. My intent for this book is to help other souls who need healing and to ignite the goddess flame, wisdom, and feminine sisterhood that are awakening.

This is a photo that I took while I was hiking in Boynton Canyon. It feels appropriate to put this photo at the end of this book. To me, it encapsulates all beings of love and light! I couldn't see this photo with my physical eyes, but I was guided to take the photo of the sun, and when I loaded the digital image onto my laptop this is the magic that appeared!

Crystal Reference for Each Goddess

Goddess Association with Crystal for Healing

Aine—Purple or Multicolored Fluorite, or Staurolite
Aphrodite—Raw Blue Aquamarine
Artemis—Black Arrowhead, Obsidian, or Orange Carnelian
Athena—Hematite
Bast—Tiger's Eye Brown or Red
Brigit—Blue Lace Agate
Butterfly Maiden—Herkimer Quartz Diamond
Coventina—Larimar
Dana—Avalon Blue Andara
Diana—Golden Topaz
Eireen—Labradorite
Green Tara—Green Aventurine or Malachite
Hathor—Red Rock from Sedona
Ishtar—Ruby
Isis—Lapis Lazuli
Isolt—Turquoise
Ixchel—Amazonite
Kali—Danburite
Kuan Yin—Rhodonite or Kyanite
Lakshmi—Citrine
Luna—Rainbow Moonstone
Maeve—Gray & White Moonstone
Mawu—Seraphinite
Mother Mary—Heart-Shaped Rose Quartz
Nemetona—Azurite
Pele—Cuprite or Divine Fire Andara
Rhiannon—Selenite

Sedna—Green Fluorite
Sekhmet—Sodalite
Sige—Sugilite
White Tara—Clear Quartz or Jade